Summons to Life

Summons to Life

The Search for Identity through the Spiritual

by

MARTIN ISRAEL, M.B.

HODDER AND STOUGHTON
LONDON SYDNEY AUCKLAND TORONTO

My thanks are due to Denis Duncan without whose encouragement and help this book would not have been written.

Contents

Prologue

I call heaven and earth to record this day against you, that I have set
before you life and death, blessing and cursing: therefore choose life.
Deuteronomy 30.19

MAN STRUGGLES TO KEEP alive, yet often forgets to live. He is
obsessed with acquiring things, yet he seldom has the time or
the understanding to enjoy them. The will to survive is a prerequisite for life, but if the object of the living is simply to
escape, or postpone, death, we are indeed truly dead already.

The time in which we live is notable for the great scientific
advances and social achievements that have swept humanity on
and transformed its members into active units. And yet the
individual is as far from true fulfilment as a person as he has
ever been. What is the measure of a truly mature person? He
is the one who is at home in the world because he is at home
in himself.

In the mad rush for security and peace, there is too often an
escape from the person to an outer world of authority, where
responsibility may be laid at the door of someone else. Yet there
can be no peace that does not come from the depths of our own
being, no security that does not arise from the love within, and
no knowledge that does not proclaim the unity of the person in
the greater community of creation.

"The glory of God is a living man" wrote St. Irenaeus some
1,800 years ago. He saw this glory in the Incarnation of Jesus
Christ. If the Incarnation has anything to say to us today, it is
to impel us onwards to something of the measure of humanity
that was in Christ. A living man is not simply a man who is
physically alive. He is a man in whom every part of the total
personality is working in co-ordination, so that he is in dynamic
relationship with the whole universe, and moving in harmony

with it to its final end in God, Who is the ultimate reality to which all sentient beings aspire.

Of course, such a vision of a living man must remain, at least at one level, a pure hypothesis. There is no certain evidence that the universe is moving towards its completion in unity with its creator. Indeed, the cataclysmic events of our own time could presage disintegration as easily as synthesis. The lives of many men, even those whom we admire most for their saintliness, often end in tragedy, so that it would seem that they have betrayed their own vision. A philosophy that sees the world as the development of random forces, and with no moral future at all other than that which man may direct from his own nature, is plausible, and indeed in some sources, popular.

The argument against a random, purposeless creation lies not in intellectual sophistry but in a deep contemplation of the course of history and the inner nature of the human being. We cannot dogmatise about the origin and destiny of the universe, but we can speak with some authority about our responses to the world we live in and the behaviour that accrues from those responses. As a man thinks in his heart, so is he. As a man is, so he orders the world around him. As he changes the world around him, so the whole complexion of society alters. When man reflects the glory of the Word of God become flesh, he lifts up the world around him and brings it nearer to its divine source. Thus we know most of God when we know ourselves best. It is the movement towards self-knowledge that brings us towards a knowledge of life.

To what does the heart vibrate in greatest acclaim? Is it wealth—which is evanescent? Is it fame—which is short-lived? Is it the opinions of others—who are fickle and self-centred? Is it power—which separates us from other people and isolates us? Or is it a will to meaning? This meaning casts a shaft of light on the dark course of personal life moving inevitably towards its end in physical death. It leads us on from physical repletion to mental growth, and from mental growth to spiritual understanding.

It is with the spirit of man that this book deals; what that spirit is and how it may be experienced are the subjects of our consideration. For it is the giver of life, and where it is there is liberty. True life is liberation from the bondage of matter to the mutual communion of all creatures in God, Who is our home.

When we know ourselves we begin to live with meaning and purpose. The world expands, and our hearts respond in joyful radiance.

This is the life abundant which alone is worth having. He who has it can never die.

CHAPTER I

The measure of a man

How DIFFICULT IT IS to define a "human being". In what does his humanity in fact consist? It cannot be confined to his body or even his reasoning mind and emotional nature. All these parts of his personality are in a state of constant change and fluctuation. In terms of the body and reasoning mind man is merely a very intelligent animal who is far better equipped than any other animal to adapt himself to outer circumstances, because of his ability to manipulate the outside world. It is when we move in awareness beyond the selfishness of immediate gratification that we begin to experience other modalities of our hidden nature.

The glory of man is his isolation in a world of private experience and his ability to work towards meaning by the use of imagination. When the mind runs free and is not engaged in mere wish-fulfilling daydreams but is focusing on the world of ideals and aspirations, a wonderful opening occurs. Enclosure is transcended by hope, and the heart expands in joyful response.

We live in a world of darkness which is illuminated by our own courageous movements towards a light, which though within us, is concealed from the eye of reason. Yet in giving of ourselves in hope beyond reason—and this is a venture of faith— we glimpse a depth of reality in ourselves which is the true self, also called the soul. What we would aspire to if we only had the wisdom to do so, would be to live under the direction of the soul, for its dominion is free and joyous.

To know your true self is life's quest. When it is known, you have indeed grown into life. But is there anything about myself that is really authentic, or am I merely the product of a number of influences working on me from outside?

That I am the result of the conditioning received from the earliest period of my life, both parental and social, is undoubted. Without the conditioning of education, I would not be able to communicate effectively with other people, nor would I be able to engage usefully in any work. Furthermore, I am the product of my animal inheritance. The impulses driving me to self-preservation and sex are strong indeed, and much of what I believe is autonomous action, is really dictated by unconscious urges and impulses.

The realm of depth psychology has explored this part of consciousness and behaviour so thoroughly that it need not be further discussed here. The great liberation of our present understanding is that the impulses derived from our animal background are not to be denied or decried. The body is indeed a sacred organism, and its growth both mirrors and modifies the development of the inner nature.

The great discovery that lies in promise for us all is the realisation of our true identity, that within each of us which is authentic. It makes itself felt during moments of choice, not the choice between two superficial actions so much as the choice between moral alternatives. The moment when I have to pass beyond the cosy existence of conforming with my social environment to a greater acknowledgment of my responsibility to the world at large is the moment of truth. There is pain for me and suffering for those about whom I care most when I make a moral decision that cuts across conformity towards the aspiration of a greater service in which I may be more fully myself. It is then that I register my authentic nature, a nature shining from the light of my soul and radiating through the trappings of personality so that the body itself is transmuted.

From all this we learn that man grows in stature through moral choice, and that the way to self-realisation is by suffering. This suffering is the result of false identification, which in turn is a product of conditioning by a society that prefers exigent advantage to spiritual enlightenment. The self that I identify in normal living is the fleeting ego that represents the present focus of my awareness. Not only is it a fluctuating point of awareness, but it is also deeply influenced by my animal inheritance from the unconscious mind and the conditioning that the environment constantly imposes on me.

It is a long way from this existential self to the true, or spiritual, self which is my real identity. The course of constructive living is to foster the light of the true self in such dedication that it may pervade the personality and raise up the ego to a consciousness of true being.

The main attributes of the soul are its all-embracing nature and its freedom within a vast range. Unlike the ego of the existential self, it is never alone or in isolation, but is in wordless communion with all other souls and with the power that transcends and infuses the world. The soul does not seek for itself alone; it is never selfish. Its joy is the joy of all the creation, and it is complete only when the whole world has moved into completion.

The body is the vehicle of the soul, and it mirrors the inner nature uncompromisingly. It is a sad thing when one is confronted by a body scarcely living, though technically fully alive, which radiates a sickly yellowish emanation from a mind full of apathy and fear. On the other hand, a body vibrant with life is a joy to behold. It speaks of a soul in command.

Not surprisingly, a soul-infused body is seen most often in little children. Subsequent experience soon dulls the soul's light and darkens the body and the mind unless love is also given to the child.

When we live in the enclosure of the personal, or existential, self we are bound to circumstances. Our lives are controlled by outer events and inner bodily and emotional disquietude. Our actions depend on the affairs of the moment or the unconscious urges and drives that are deep within us. There is no freedom of inner choice, only a makeshift selection of possible responses to an overwhelming external presence that menaces us. When we live in the consciousness of the personal self, we work only to survive, but survival has the sole virtue of delaying death with its apparent annihilation of all we know. This is not the life that man was destined to lead. He has fallen from his high place in the hierarchy of nature. He has quitted his birthright, and has sacrificed his leadership of the world in order to gain comfort through possessions. The more insecure we are, the more we need to possess, to own, to master intellectually and emotionally. The freer we are in security, the less need have we for possessions, and the more aware are we of a constant relationship with the outside world that is consecrated to a mutual concern that unites commitment with freedom. The more I need to have, the less I am. The less concerned I am about my attributes and the more I flow out from the soul to the world, the richer I am. I am no longer merely myself; I embrace the other also as it embraces me. We are no longer entirely separate, but through the inner sharing we are both enriched to a greater experience of our true being.

If the other is a person, there is a communion of souls and a new birth into a greater reality for both. But even if the other is merely an object, it is still enriched by my love of it. This is the mystery of resurrection into life by a true relationship.

As I grow into a deeper awareness of what I might become if I were less self-enclosed, so I become more sensitive to the onward flowing power that pulsates through my personality and gives me full life. This is the spirit within me. It is the lord of my life, but usually I am so worn down by the cares, stresses, and exigencies of mortal life that I am scarcely aware of its promptings. When, however, I am tractable to a greater reality than myself, the spirit within me illuminates my soul, and gives me an intimation of the path to the life of abundance. It can, through a special grace, illuminate my mind with a knowledge of the being of God, and so lead me on to the most exciting quest in life, the spiritual ascent. This is the movement of the soul towards its fullness of being in God, Who makes Himself known to us in the highest point of the soul, called the spark, or apex, or better still the spirit. In or through His Spirit, God makes His immanence, or indwelling nature, known to us.

The Spirit leads us into the truth about ourselves. When we are divested of personal craving, the spirit, which is of God, directs the whole personality Godward, but in the early stages of our awareness, when selfishness is uppermost, the power of the spirit is perverted into paths of self-seeking and aggrandisement. The path of man to the recognition of his spirit is the spiritual path, and spirituality is the movement of the personality to God. To move into spiritual reality is man's true end in life, for only in such reality is man authentic. To be oneself fully and gloriously is the greatest joy you can know, for at last you are free. This freedom is gained at a heavy price, but only when you are free can you enjoy your own being as well as the world around you. Thus man's concern for spirituality, often mistakenly equated with religion, speaks of the inner acknowledgment of his true nature and of his destination.

How can we move to a knowledge of God, Who alone can fill us with that meaning in life which makes all difficulties appear as nothing compared with His radiance? The answer is simple. It is by living in awareness of the moment and responding positively to the challenge of relationships with those around us. This is the basis of spirituality. It is no longer to be thought of as something reserved only for those who have dedicated their lives to silent contemplation in a religious community. The dedication is as fundamental as ever, but in the contemporary scene we have to participate actively in and partake wholeheartedly of every episode of the passing scene of life.

It is in the depths of the living mass that we glimpse the mountain of transfiguration. The journey downwards into our own inner nature is also the way to God. Nothing is valueless to him who can discern the divinity that manifests itself in all its creation.

In this realised divinity there is eternal joy.

CHAPTER 2

The point of departure

WHERE DO WE START on the spiritual journey? What is our point of departure? or put the question in this form—when does the intimation of the reality of the spirit occur in our lives?

There is no single answer to this question. A child is, in many ways, more aware of the wonders of the world around him than he will be some years later when the unavoidable impact of conditioning by his social environment dulls his inner sensitivity and draws him closer to the illusions of material things. But this is not the whole answer. The process of growing into life is one in which all the powers inherent in the personality are progressively realised in the actions of life. The child is in direct contact with a world of spiritual reality, but he is a passive spectator. The experience of life brings him into active relationship with that reality, so that he may eventually be consciously part of it.

In living, the first impulse is to survive in an environment that is often indifferent to us and sometimes very hostile to us. There can be no growth into humanity until the prerequisites of bodily survival and satisfaction have been met. Thus a growing person becomes increasingly concerned about his own well-being, and the process of education develops his personality to its peak of efficiency. But in addition to this there is the need to be acknowledged as a person, and this should take place when we are still little children. The fact that we are recognised as individual persons, each with his own name, is the beginning of the realisation of personal integrity and responsibility.

Many children are not confirmed as persons in this way. They are not acknowledged as individuals by their parents, and they have great difficulty in finding their own identity. It is no exaggeration to say that the greatest problem that afflicts us in the world today is a crisis of identity—personal, national, and global. We do not really know who we are or what the purpose of our existence is.

It is the love of the parent that first affirms the unique identity of his child. The quest for love and its final manifestation in the freedom of the spirit is the whole path of spiritual development. Growth into the fullness of life is also a graduated exploration into the meaning and power of love.

The love that identifies each person as something unique and valuable in his own right is a love that strives for the survival of that person and that works for his own growth into fullness of being. In the early stages of life this love is experienced from outside, and is the true intimation of love. It always comes first to us. If we know of love and are sure we are cared for, we have a direct proof that we matter as people, and therefore that our identity is real. Of course, this view of identity is still superficial and simple. It is a selfish view based on the conception that we are all-important, and that the concern of those about us should revolve around us. Such self-centredness is the natural awareness of the contented child. He is also in inner communion with nature around him. This is a glorious state, but also a primitive one. It belongs more to our animal inheritance than our human destiny. Why is it inadequate? Because it depends entirely on the equable disposition of the outside world, and it can be destroyed in a single moment by a change in those outside circumstances. It is man's work on himself that is to bring him into a communion with all things that can never be destroyed. To know peace in chaos, joy in suffering, immortality in death is the destiny of a fully realised man. This work brings us into union with Him Who is the Master, the Overseer, of the work, Whom we know as God.

The growth into the fullness of our own being is a growing into a progressively greater knowledge of the being of God. Such a knowledge is not one that is externally imposed but one that is learned from inner experience. This experience demands the consecration of every part of the personality—body, reasoning mind, and emotions, as well as soul and spirit—to the great quest. It does not demand subjection or denial of any part of our

being, but rather a full, joyous participation of the whole personality in the glorious encounter. There are no pre-conditions other
than a humble receptivity to life and a faith that persists in
adversity, of which I shall have more to say later.

The realisation of your true identity consists primarily in de-
taching yourself from those attributes that are superficial but
which you, in your blind ignorance, consider essential to your
being. In other words, the movement towards the real is first
and foremost a progressive stripping from yourself of illusions.
This stripping is never really voluntary. It comes to us through
those events we call tragedies, or, at the very least, disappoint-
ments. We would not seek the real, the unchangeable, the reliable
if we could live happily in the world of illusion with all its
glamour and false security. But the course of life is punctuated
by episodes, not infrequently of long duration, in which those
things we have held dear are taken from us. It may be the wealth
of a rich man, or the life of one who is dear to us, or our health,
or even our reputation. It may be the work that sustained us, or
even a special gift on which we relied. In some people's lives
there has been very little experience of love. It might be thought
therefore that such people would be incapable of giving love or
even of recognising it, and yet this very dereliction can serve
a purpose in directing the person's attention to his true condition.

It is far worse to live an anonymous life, even on the crest of
a wave of material success and affluence, than to be aware of your
true identity though in a state of destitution. In this latter contin-
gency you are at least down to bare essentials, and the rock of
true being is the foundation-stone of a new life. The role of
suffering in the growth of personality cannot be over-emphasised,
but it all depends on the view one has about suffering and how
best it should be confronted.

It is no use telling someone who is in severe distress that it
is all useful experience for the growth of his own soul. Years
can be spent in fighting against a multitude of misfortunes, and
one's life can ultimately expire with the mumbled cursing of
the personality against the whole cosmic process. Yet such a
person may be nearer the great discovery of his own true being
than one who is shielded against adversity by pleasant outer
circumstances. The key to the disclosure of inner reality is always
the tacit admission that we of ourselves can do nothing, that

the process of our intellects comes to a humiliating halt, and that we are creatures of darkness surrounded by an even denser obscurity. It is the courage to admit our ignorance and impotence that is the key which opens a new dimension of reality to us. No wonder God told Dame Julian of Norwich that sin is necessary but that finally all will be well.

Sin is man's natural state. It is a condition in which we exalt our own self-interest above that of the greater community of man and nature, even to the detriment of the greater good. The Biblical story of the fall of man, though surely a parable, nevertheless stresses that when man was granted the knowledge of duality—of good and evil—his free will was sharpened and realised. He could now work for or against the cosmic purpose of the living God, and could come back to the Creator only by willed effort. This is the deeper significance of the evolutionary process, that the human creature might re-establish communion with the Creator as a fully responsible agent infused with the power of God, who had never really left him, but who insisted that he should make real the divinity which was inherent in him. Not for nothing was it said that man was created in the image of God. But for this image, imprinted deep in the soul as the spirit, to be made a living reality, man must work in collaboration with God.

It is the nature of this collaboration that marks out the spiritual life. The essence of the human and divine collaboration is that God never makes man's path easy or lifts the various obstacles and burdens on the way, but that He infuses man with strength and illumination to guide him to self-mastery.

Laws of the spiritual nature

There are laws of the spiritual nature which are worth considering. One is that *every petition made in faith is heard and answered*. The answer is frequently not obvious at once, but it sets in action a train of events that are seen in retrospect to have changed the whole tenor and progress of a life. Not for nothing has it been promised that in asking we shall receive and in knocking it shall be opened to us. What is needed from us in this transaction is faith; not the belief that the request is already granted despite all external evidence to the contrary, but a forging ahead despite all difficulties while knowing that help is coming to us in order to sustain our faltering steps.

Another spiritual law is that *all creatures live in psychic communion,* and that any sinful action—that is, one that exalts the individual over and above his fellows—excludes him from the spirit of life that animates the world. This is the Holy Spirit, the Lord and Giver of life. We are indeed all members one of another, and anything I do contrary to nature, and more especially anything hurtful to a fellow human being, cuts me off from psychic communion with him. This is the sin against the Holy Spirit, and I am literally in a state of hell until I confess my fault and ask forgiveness. If I, through pride or sheer ignorance, persist in my intransigence, I shall exclude myself from the greater community of life, and eventually my mind and body will suffer.

It is not improbable that such a psychic dysfunction may be the factor that predisposes to much illness that may be caused by other, more tangible agents that would normally have been successfully repelled. The more sensitive and spiritually awake I am, the sooner will be my realisation of the error of my way, and the more rapidly will I be compelled to confess and repent. But if I am thick-skinned and obtuse, I may persist in a state of sin for many years, gradually alienating all those around me so that I become thoroughly isolated. The effect of this on the development of my personality is not hard to imagine.

It is a strange paradox that the further I grow into maturity the less do I rely entirely on my own talents and the more do I open myself to that which is beyond me, yet intimately concerned in my progress. This invocation of the power beyond me, which transforms me and makes me an ever more useful servant, is both my initial and final encounter with God, who is defined as *that which is.* As I grow more into my true being, so does the fact of God impinge itself more and more intensely on my awareness. Thus God, far from being an idolised father-figure projected by the unconscious of an immature person who cannot face the facts of life on his own, is the source and destination of my growth into full humanity.

The more I acknowledge my weakness, the stronger do I become. The more I realise that of myself I can do nothing, the greater the burden of work I can perform without fatigue or mental breakdown. The fruit of spirituality is an analysis of our various attributes so that the one unfailing quality in us can be revealed. This is our true self, or soul, for there God is immanent as (or through) the spirit, from which the Holy Spirit emanates to lead the whole personality into that truth which alone can set us free from dependence on all things that are not God.

It must, however, be said that not all growing into spirituality is accompanied by violent tragedy and a progressive loss of all that is not essential. It also comes about by active, harmonious participation in the round of everyday activity. It may be that in playing our unpretentious part in the daily task we also see something of the process that guides the surface events, of the meaning that underlies the phenomena of nature. God reveals Himself to us in all guises provided we have the courtesy to pay attention.

We must now try to find out where and when enlightenment comes.

CHAPTER 3

The vale of enlightenment

THE KNOWLEDGE OF TRUE being comes to us in the place where we are working. It comes as a thief in the night, when we are least expecting it. It transforms our conception of reality. The key to this knowledge is *awareness*. Where we can keep our minds still, the knowledge of God can come to us. The spiritual ascent is, in essence, one of inner tranquillity in which we may become attuned to the voice of the soul within us.

The inner stillness is not to be relegated merely to periods of prayerful meditation. Indeed, meditation can easily degenerate into a technique whereby we escape the threats and demands of an ever-challenging world. The stillness that is worth having is one that is with us in the clamour of the day's work. God makes His presence real to us when the mind is aware of itself and is not merely dissipating its energy on vain thoughts and futile imaginings.

The place of suffering in our spiritual development has already been mentioned. In such a state we are fully aware of our dereliction, and our mind is resting on this painful consideration. Or the awareness of sin may become so overwhelming in the course of a religious meeting that the necessity for a complete change in outlook then becomes obvious to us. Or the mind may be lost in the inexpressible beauty of a landscape, the ineffable radiance of a great work of art, or the self-transcending devotion that occurs between two people who really care for each other. All this is meditation in everyday life. When the awareness of the mind transcends the isolation of the personal self, it establishes an intimate relationship with the other, so that it is no longer merely a subject–object communication. This communication is one in which perceiver and perceived, thinker and thought, subject and object are united into a single all-pervading reality in which duality, or separation, is lost.

As I lose my isolated self in an awareness that stretches me in commitment to the other, so I find my true self, which is in intimate communion with all other selves, and yet more truly itself than ever before. The release from the bondage of self-centred isolation is the first real experience of liberty that the person can know, a release that is not an escape from the world, but rather a deep identification of the self with the world. Thus is proved by experience Jesus' paradoxical statement that he who would save his life shall lose it, but he who loses his life for the sake of the Christ and His gospel shall have the eternal life that comes from the true realising of identity.

This experience of the soul is also an inner confirmation that we are all members one of another. Only in isolated self-awareness does my separation from the world become overwhelming. Once I ascend from the personal self to the soul, I know that I can never be alone, because I am now one with the cosmic process and all it embraces. It is in this way that a glimpse of the larger hope of salvation is bestowed on me. This knowledge does not come by direct seeking. The more avidly one presses for personal enlightenment, the more certain is one to be disappointed, or, worse still, severely deluded by psychic impressions of dubious character. Courses aimed at self-development along an allegedly spiritual path may cultivate certain psychic faculties, and indeed enhance the person's power over others, but there is no spirituality involved in this. Anything that boosts the personality separates the individual from the greater community of mankind. Anything that leads to the unveiling of the true self, or soul, diminishes the claims of the personality and brings the person into fuller communion with the process of life.

The first manifestation of this communion is an attitude of harmlessness. Indeed, the two essential preconditions for love are awareness of the other and a reverence for his identity that will do him no hurt. The less full of our own true being we are, the more we have need of an exalted personality. This means that we grasp selfishly for those attributes we lack. The more we acquire, however, the further away we are from the centre of our being, which is the soul. Once we have the centre, we can take

the periphery for granted, and flow out in the radiance of light
to those around us.

"He who has the Son has life," says St. John in his first letter.
We all have the Son, who is the inner Christ in potentiality, but
only a few are aware of Him. It is these who can be witnesses to
the Light of the World within that illuminates the world without.

True illumination comes therefore by grace and not by direct
effort. Yet grace will never act on an unprepared person. And
that preparation is one of active work in the world so that one's
very being is dedicated to one's fellow men. When the whole
personality is thus consecrated to one's neighbour, God, Who is
in all things, and between all things, and above all things, can
make His presence known to us. Then at last we are no longer
alone. The silent meaninglessness of selfish private life is extended to embrace a knowledge of purpose. Moreover we are aware
of a cloud of witnesses about us, who are the fruit of mankind.
The preparation thus needed for us to be tractable to the divine
encounter by which we know God is a consecration of every part
of ourselves to His service in the world.

This is the second great commandment, namely that we must
love our neighbour as ourself. But there can be no conception
of the real meaning of love until we can understand the first
great commandment, that we must love God with all our heart,
and mind, and soul, and strength. Only when we know of this
love that God has bestowed on us, can we start to love those
around us. Yet paradoxically, it is in conscious relationships with
others that we usually become aware of God. No wonder the
second commandment is an essential extension of the first.

The presence of God

The awareness of God is not the completion of the spiritual
path. It is merely an important milestone along it. We progress
in life by faith that the better will prevail against the worse and
that life will triumph over death. Often our faith is sorely taxed,
but we persist, driven as much by the body's desire to survive
as by the soul's hidden will to meaning. At last, often when we
are strained to the limits of our endurance, or sometimes when
we are in great peace, He comes to us, and the way to meaning is
revealed.

Whatever is said about God is wrong, for He transcends all
categories so that even a compendium of every virtue would

belittle Him. Though the Godhead is beyond human imagining, yet He comes to us as a person among persons, until He has lifted us out of our own enclosed personality so that we may begin to have a mature intimation of His full nature. God is known to us in the experience of our own souls. Without that experience, He is merely an intellectual hypothesis or a theological construction. It is His manifestation to us that brings us closer to Him, and the validity of that experience is judged by the degree of proximity that flows between Him and us.

The first intimation of divine reality is the experience of an opening-up of the enclosed personality. This can never be done by a mere act of will. It comes suddenly from outside and impinges on our awareness, which is transformed. It is as if another modality of consciousness takes control of our senses. This awareness is formless and ineffable. It is not a mere psychic interference in which forms of communication from another source come to us. The awareness of God is an awareness of warmth that permeates the very depth of our being. It speaks to us of a power beyond thought that cares for us as we are, that loves us for what we are. It is not that we feel greater love for others so much as that we are the receivers of ineffable love.

This warmth opens the "eye" of the soul to the potentialities within the person. Faith, once hidden and obscure, is now illuminated by hope that springs from this gift of love. *I* am loved for what *I* am, and *my* sins are forgiven *me*. This does not mean that the past and all its consequences cease to exist, but rather that they are no longer facts of imprisonment and condemnation. Instead, they are experiences that can lead to the fullness of life by the lessons they teach and the compassion they engender towards others. It therefore follows that in our apprehension of the divine, the aspect of personality is important. This justifies the use of the personal pronoun to describe God—though it is more questionable whether the masculine qualities rather than the feminine should be exalted in the pronoun commonly used.

This type of experience is not only a glimpse of the love of the personal God—God showing Himself to us in terms of personality, of which love is the supreme quality. It is also a view of our soul and its interconnexion with the soul of humanity and of all creation. What is now important is the proper evaluation of this manifestation of divine grace, so that it may lead us into ever-widening truth; otherwise we may, through restricted reasoning, limit the experience and derive a constricting dogma from it.

When the experience of God's love comes to someone at the emotional peak of a revivalistic meeting in which sin is loudly denounced and lamented, the release from the spiritual bondage of his special sin may easily lead the person to believe that this forgiveness is dependent on a rigid theological position that must be dogmatically upheld at all costs. Thus God's grace is conditional on our acceptance of Him in terms of a particular religious insight or tradition. The result of this is that the vision of God may easily be transformed into an imprisoning proposition that cuts one off from the body of mankind, and separates one into a small class of the elect, or the "saved". This is where an understanding of the love of God and His providence in the world is so important. God's revelation of Himself to us is progressive. Indeed, in Christian terms it is the Holy Spirit that is to lead us into all truth.

This progressive revelation by the Holy Spirit, Who is deep within us in the spirit of the soul, leads us into an ever-deepening awareness of the divinity that lies at the heart of all creation and was supremely revealed in the juxtaposition of God and man in the incarnational event. But if we are ever unwise enough to believe that we have the whole answer to God's being, we at once shut Him out of our lives, replacing Him with an idol, which may be theological, ritual, or intellectual, and which ultimately degenerates into a superstition.

On the other hand, the early revelations of God's love are as valid as the later ones. Nothing that is given at any time, that is truly of God, can be anything other than perfect. It is our own growth into greater awareness that enables God to come closer to us and show Himself ever more clearly to us. The spiritual path becomes clear and defined when the personal God reveals Himself to us. This is our initiation into the life of the spirit.

It is now that the test of our integrity commences, and wisdom is granted in every action of life. As we move beyond the limitations of our own personality to the vast reaches of the soul that underlie it, so the being of God ceases to be merely personal, but expands to embrace the whole universe, and transcend it at the same time. And the potential hope of partaking of the divine nature, that lies within all men, becomes ever closer to realisation.

The dynamics of salvation

To the more simple aspirant, salvation is a state of purification which occurs suddenly and is complete once it is accepted and the theological implications are fully acknowledged. Such a salvation puts the recipient into the category of the saved—the sheep —who are rigidly separated from those who are not saved—the goats. Such a view of salvation is uncharitable at its very least, and obviously very inadequate if the fruits of this "salvation" are studied in everyday life. The "saved" are above all else priggish, superior in attitude, and condescending in approach to their unsaved fellows. They have a definite code of rules regarding belief and behaviour, which, if followed, they are sure will lead them straight to God Himself. They are not aloof from their unfortunate brethren, however, for they are usually imbued with intense missionary zeal. Yet you sometimes feel that the desire to win converts is as much to assuage unconscious doubts about the reality of the scheme of salvation of that body as to help others to a fuller, more abundant life. The limitation of this view of salvation is not in the reality of the initial experience of God's grace, but in the finality of the vision of God that the aspirant deduces from that experience.

True salvation is to be seen as the healing of the whole person. This means an integration of the personality so that the body, reasoning mind, and emotional nature are working under the conscious direction of the soul, which is itself illuminated by the Spirit, Who is God immanent. This salvation is a slow but progressive process. It is punctuated by many episodes of failure and apparent regression, which in turn are the portals of entry for God's mysterious grace which reveals new aspects of the divine love to us. Thus the first experience of God's personal presence is followed by a penetration of the darkness that is both of the world and in our own unconscious minds.

It is no surprise that Christ spent time in the wilderness after His baptism and the descent of the Holy Spirit upon Him. It is in the redemption of the most sordid aspects of creation that we can see the scale of salvation, which can only be complete for the person when it embraces all people. The path of salvation is one of a rugged journey across the valley of desolation, up the hills of vision, and eventually to the mountain of transfiguration. The hallmark of the right path is the progressive loss of self-concern—indeed of the awareness of separate self—that becomes ever more obvious to others as one proceeds onwards. This is a far cry from the arrogant self-assurance of the instantly saved who is so superior in his own eyes to the remainder of humanity that he resembles the Pharisee who thanked God that he was not as other men were, particularly the publican. And yet it was the self-reproachful publican who left God justified, for the Pharisee had hardly yet begun to know the God whom he thanked with such self-satisfaction.

The beginning of this process of healing is facing oneself in candid awareness, not flinching from the dark and formidable elements of the unconscious. This means in effect an active participation in the round of common life. Our true nature with its many imperfections impinges upon us in our attitudes to other people and the events of the world around us. The abundant life depends first on a progressive recognition of the material in the unconscious and then its active integration in the conscious life of the person. The pain experienced in this journey of self-discovery is often very great, but when it is almost too great to bear, the love of God breaks into our consciousness, showing us more of the divine reality. It is in this way that the personality is resurrected.

This self-discovery comes to us in the life of the world around us. It needs no special efforts to encompass it, nor need we go to far-away places to find it. Indeed, it requires far greater spiritual dedication to reach the centre of being in a large, noisy modern city than in some place of refuge in the mountains. The value of such places of refuge is that one can gain equilibrium in a quiet atmosphere, but in due course one has to return to the greater world once more.

There are some inevitable circumstances of life that impinge on us so intimately that we cannot fail to react to them and thereby see more clearly into ourselves. These are firstly relationships with other people, secondly the course of our chosen work, and lastly the fact of suffering which is a part of our limitation in a time–space universe.

To these we must now turn.

CHAPTER 4

Spiritual growth in everyday life

THE LIVES OF MOST aspirants swing between the two extremes of deep contemplation and active work in the world. It might be argued that this split in emphasis in itself rules out real spiritual progress. In most of the higher religions there is a special path set out for those attempting the spiritual, or mystical, life. Religious communities exist where the whole purpose is the life in God. Here the inner disciplines of prayer and meditation juxtapose themselves in a communal setting, and in aligning himself to other members of the community, the aspirant gains knowledge of himself both in silence and in conversation. The secular life is, in fact, not greatly different, except that the time available for silent communion is considerably less than in a religious community, and the challenge of outer events is much greater. Yet in all the world, the place of action of any person is restricted to the locality and the people whom he may meet. The ministry of Christ was confined to the small area of Palestine, and the Buddha served only in a limited part of India. Yet their impact has changed the face of the world. Whenever a secular aspirant becomes disheartened by the hostile environment in which he lives, he is well advised to meditate on the witness of the great ones of this world. Their circumstances were also far from satisfactory, and most of those who heard them had no real understanding of their teaching.

It is all too easy to blame our particular circumstances for our lack of advancement. How can I aspire to spiritual knowledge when I am confronted day after day with some uninspiring routine work among companions whose awareness seldom rises above mundane sensual impressions? This is a constant problem, and it must be faced at the outset.

Let us first remember that most adult work has a routine, somewhat stereotyped character. The factory worker turns out the same product, the laboratory technician performs a restricted number of tests, the cobbler works on shoes, the housewife is engaged in unexciting household duties, and so it goes on. Even professions that seem to be more stimulating, for instance medicine or the law, involve much wearisome routine work. In fact, no work can provide constant stimulation unless the person is himself involved in it. This is the key to spiritual growth in the world—an attitude of detached awareness combined with a commitment to give of one's utmost to the work at hand. It is not the nature of the work that ultimately matters; it is the dedication of the worker that determines how much he gives of himself and how much benefit he derives from it.

In the daily task we are continually being confronted by the self, especially the unconscious part which impinges on our consciousness when anything disturbs the equilibrium of the moment. Much of our time is taken up with various unprofitable flights of ideas into past reminiscences and regrets and future forebodings. A train of thought often follows a particular event in our lives, the association of which recalls a past emotional response. The result of all this is that we are not devoting our full attention to our work, but are instead expending emotional energy on mental images that dominate our attention.

One of the worst sources of such emotional depletion is a state of enmity with another person. Here our whole attention is dominated by imaginary confrontations, and while the course of the present moment passes by we are completely engrossed in ideas of self-justification or revenge. The mind can certainly rob us of true peace if it is allowed to take over the course of our lives.

In order to prevent this internal corruption that spoils our lives, a state of *willed awareness* is essential. We have to recognise what is happening, and resolve to keep the mind at rest on the work at hand. If only we had the childlike simplicity to await each moment as it came, we would find the divine presence in that moment leading us into greater truth about ourselves. This is not merely an introspective analysis of our own reactions to the flux of outer events, but rather an active participation in those events, so that a synthesis of ourselves and the impact of the events can occur. This manifests itself as a raising of the level of awareness. The more actively we strain to be aware of the moment to the exclusion of past regrets and future fears, the more certainly we shall fail. The psychic fatigue that such an effort engenders will lead us to relax our intention quickly, and once more we shall be lost in useless daydreams, reminiscences, and regrets. The way to achieve this equilibrium in balance is by flowing out to the source of the work, Who is God the Creator.

It is important that our attention should rest on *the work*, so that the effort expended actually diminishes instead of increasing. The right approach is to rest while working vigorously, to relax in the heat of activity, to be fully oneself as one is lost in the greater glory of the universe.

It is often stated that tension is essential for really creative work, and this is sometimes held to imply that difficult circumstances, whether bodily, personal, or financial, are necessary to stimulate the creative drive. But tension is the inevitable state of man while he is incarnate. The limitation of a time–space world on the vast amount of work that a creative individual is empowered to do is a sufficient basis of tension to stimulate this creative potentiality. This type of tension is healthy and an inevitable part of life in the world. The tensions that arise as a result of a malalignment of the personal will with the flow of the cosmos (or with God's will, as a religionist would put it) lead to mental aberration, personal antagonisms, and physical ill-health. While these conditions are by no means incompatible with creative performance, they often show themselves as imbalance, disharmony, and emotional turmoil. The key to a real unfolding of latent talents is a state of balance. Once there is outer calm and inner tranquillity, the work of the Holy Spirit, Who is the source of inspiration, can proceed through an efficient organism.

Meditation in action

There are, of course, times when things appear to go wrong despite all reason. A person who tries to regulate his life by the power of the intellect soon learns what an insignificant part the rational categories play. It is the unexpected, the untoward, that is the real master of events, and by its very nature it cannot be predicted and anticipated. Yet if we live in active awareness of each moment of life taken as a sacrament, we are in a state of complete self-control, so that we can meet the challenge of the unexpected with remarkably acute presence of mind. And if the circumstance is something unpleasant, like a disappointment or some physical illness, we can accept it as a new trial and event, which is part of the process of self-revelation.

This is called *meditation in action* in the Buddhist tradition. It does not mean a spineless resignation to every adverse outer event as part of God's inscrutable will, but rather an active participation in that event so that through a willed giving of oneself, the meaning behind the event can be dimly but definitely divined. Thus does God reveal Himself ever more clearly as the universal source of strength to all who call upon Him when they are fully taxed. It is in our weakness that He comes. He asks no questions, demands no credal passport, but only needs our desperate searchings for reality. While we are lost in vain thoughts, He cannot come near us. But when we are empty of vanity, we are in a state of readiness to be filled by the Holy Spirit.

This is what active work in the world has to teach us about reality. Every moment of the dreariest routine work is an opening to the divine grace provided we rest on the work and do not lose ourselves in other thoughts. Indeed, the right state of mind in which to receive the divine visitor is one of clear, alert passivity. A mind that is quiet and at peace is one that is not thinking discursively but rather waiting expectantly. We think far too much about trivialities when it would be much better that we ceased all thought and waited in expectancy for the Son of God to appear in all His glory. If the mind were habitually quiet and rested, it would be able to think deeply, constructively, and unemotionally when deep thoughts and far-reaching decisions are really necessary. On the other hand, a mind that is constantly flitting round in inconsequential tracks is inefficient and emotionally unbalanced. When an urgent decision is necessary, it is so overwhelmed by a confusion of impressions that it fails to come to any clear answer.

This state of active passivity, or detached commitment, is the very heart of the spiritual life. Until it is understood clearly, there can be no real love for another—emotional need and clinging certainly, but not real love. This is a hard saying, but one that cannot be overemphasised. It is only when we know the love of God that comes in the stillness that we can flow out in that stillness to another person. When we know that peace and can bequeath it to another, we are beginning to love that person very deeply. The fruit of work is the acceptance of the action as a guide to divine grace. The results of the action are not our business; it is only the perfection of the act that lies within our scope. The hardest problem that confronts us in work is coming to the right decision. It is the approach to this problem that indicates the reality of spiritual growth most clearly.

When we try to reach a decision about a particular course of action we naturally hope to do what is best for ourselves and others too. This means that we look for a favourable result which will bring gain and success to us. But what do we know of success? The little preview of future happiness that is vouchsafed us at the summit of a decision gives us no intimation of the wider issues in the more distant future. Every action is followed by a train of events, some of which are pleasant and others unpleasant. The gifts that are bestowed on us as a part of our natural inheritance will, if used in quiet, unemotional detachment, lead us along the path of least pain. By this I mean that if we use the reasoning mind, the feeling nature, and the body's dictates, properly, we will not move blindly into a destructive action. But none of these guides can lead us into eternal happiness. In front of us lies the dark abyss of future ignorance, and it is faith, not reason, that leads us through the valley of the shadow of death.

It is in passing through this inevitable valley of decision and dereliction that we learn the nature of our sustenance. The sustainer is not our reason or even our intuition. It is a power from without that guides us with that personal detachment, that passive concern, that universal particularity which is of the nature of love. *God* is His name. Thus the important factor in making any decision is not so much the outer result that accrues from that decision as the attitude of complete dedication of the self that follows the act of deciding and carrying out the work.

Ideas of good and evil, essential as they are for the even performance of the day's work, are merely relative. As we grow in spiritual knowledge, so our conception of the good increases, and we live less in terms of duality and more in willed union with all things. Thus an enlightened tolerance which is the result of deeper compassion and increasing knowledge moves us on to an ever-widening relationship with all aspects of the world around us. Compassion changes evil to good, whereas condemnation merely hardens and crystallises the evil impulse.

When we live in the moment of creative life, the dictates of the personality with its resentment, pride, envy, and hatred of others more favoured with special talents than ourselves are encompassed in a wider thanksgiving that flows out from the soul. We thank God for what we are and what we have in that moment of time. For it is the moment of God also.

As we obey the summons to life, we come face to face with that most fundamental experience, Love. Let us now consider its nature.

CHAPTER 5

The mystery of love

LOVE IS THE KEYSTONE of the arch that joins the soul to God. Its apprehension is the very heart of the spiritual journey, and its consummation brings us to God Himself. It is important to trace the course of love from its beginnings to its final fruits, for in its working lies the meaning and destiny of all created things.

Man is never complete when he is alone. It is natural for him to assuage his loneliness in the company of other people. There comes a time in the lives of most young people when a sudden irrational attraction draws them to someone else, usually of the opposite sex. This is, of course, described as "falling in love". Its momentum is so violent that the emotions drive the person to union with the beloved against all rational judgment. Such a state of loving is as much physiological as psychological, so it is a most important milestone in the development of the personality of most (but not all) people.

The beauty of this condition and its importance in the spiritual path is that it releases the person's concern from his own well-being and projects it on to the beloved. Thus there is a temporary release of the personality, and the soul can show its light. Life takes on a new meaning; the old ways are dead and all around is bliss. It is no wonder that much of the world's greatest poetry has been written in the glow of great love, while some of this forms the basis of the treasury of song.

But falling in love, though in one way a liberating experience, is also a confusing and even a deluding one. Since the reasoning mind is subjugated by the uninhibited flow of emotion that is released from the unconscious mind, its judgment is eclipsed. Furthermore, much of the unfulfilled longing that lies deep in us is projected on to the beloved, who therefore appears to possess all those attributes that we ourselves so desperately lack. In a very real way, though there is intimate involvement between lover and beloved, there is remarkably little real relationship, for each is more aware of the ideal that is seen in the other than in the reality that in truth exists. This reality is much more obvious to detached observers. It is easy to be cynical about young love, but it is wrong—on every level. When the young fall in love they are proclaiming their own ideals. Romantic love is always beautiful because it is spontaneous, unreserved, and, in the highest meaning of that word, innocent. Until you are a fool in love, you cannot know your own depths fully, and therefore you remain enclosed—"safe" certainly but also isolated. Until you give yourself, and suffer betrayal if need be, you cannot know what the soul is and what of yourself can never be lost. A fool in love is also a fool for God. Whatever is lost is repaid by increased self-knowledge.

The one certain attribute of romantic love is its transience. If it is not deepened into a more durable practical love it is liable to be dissipated, and transferred to someone else. This is indeed the course of love for most young people, but there comes a time when something more substantial is needed. This has to be honest. It is now that love comes into its mature manifestation. In order that this may occur, the very practical marriage relationship has been devised by generations of people of different religious and racial backgrounds. When love is anchored down into the realities of everyday life and enclosed in a duration of permanence, it loses much of its glamour. The beloved is seen more clearly as he (or she) really is, and the lover's reaction to this unadorned vision gives him (or her) a new insight into the nature of his (or her) own soul. This is the moment of truth when glamorous communication is extended into a mundane relationship. It is also the paradigm of the impetuous conversion experience, when one is full of God's love, which has to be extended into less joyful secular life, when the awareness of divine grace fades and one proceeds by faith rather than direct vision.

A constant relationship where the very depths of one's personality are exposed to the critical, and often hostile, scrutiny of the other is both a fearful experience and a healing one. If we live in awareness of the situation and face the unpleasant facts about our own selfishness and moral dishonesty with equanimity, we learn more and more about ourselves and can begin to accept much, both in ourselves and in others, that would previously have been unbearable. It is, in fact, very hard for a person to understand relationships until he has given of himself to another in his very life. Those who do not need marriage to establish a pattern of right relationships will be found to be advanced souls in whom celibacy means a perfect harmonisation of the various facets of their own personalities. On the other hand, there are many marriages, perhaps even the majority of marriages, in which a true relationship never develops between man and wife. The union is one of worldly convenience and not of spiritual growth. The partners simply do not know each other.

How beautiful a real marriage is to behold! The man and the woman glow in deep serenity. The growth of both from inexperienced youth to calm, yet masterful, maturity is a glorious thing. The girl becomes a fulfilled woman and the man flourishes in his worldly profession. But more than these outer manifestations of successful living, there is an inner spiritual emanation that makes each of them a focus of light and healing for all the world around them. In other words, the proof of a real and growing love between two people is the radiation of that love to the whole world, so that more and more people are embraced in the outflowing concern of the lovers, whose awareness transcends their family to encompass a greater family of men. Thus does love which starts on a personal, rather exclusive level expand into a living union with all created things.

Unfortunately, not all lovers experience this fullness of relationship. Many become so attached to one another that each life is lost in the other, and there is no growth into maturity. They are certainly in love with each other, but also chained in an attachment that leaves neither free. A selfishness extends from one person to encompass the two in close union, and the rest of the world is of no account to them. In due course one of the partners must die, and then the other is left disconsolate. While mourning after the death of a loved one is a most natural circumstance, if this mourning continues indefinitely, to the detriment of the growth of the remaining person, the relationship that was enjoyed previously cannot be regarded as a con-

structive one. It becomes clear that the whole basis of living
was an attachment to one other person.

In this type of union, you can lose your own identity and
even your personal responsibility in the beloved, only to realise
that you have not grown into an independent person when bereft
of the support for which you had previously lived. What passes
as love can be emotional coercion by one person on another; it can
also be an escape from reality into a private world of mutual
adulation and comfort. And once again the counterpart of vain
human attachment is mirrored in immature attitudes towards
God. The immature may love a god who demands complete
obedience from them according to the precepts of some spiritual authority; if they transgress these precepts, they can expect
punishment from this vengeful potentate. Alternatively, religion
can be a glorious escape from the stresses of the world into
some private domain of the elect who live in constant communication with the Almighty. He speaks directly to them, tells them
what to do, and leads them into all material blessings—to the
cost of their own growth into mature human beings.

It follows from this that what the world speaks of as love
is usually merely an emotional response of need by immature
people. What they lack in themselves they seek in other people,
and the attraction, which can assume a python-like strangle-
hold, leads ultimately to a diminution of the personality of all
concerned. How different was the love of Christ—and to a more
limited extent that of the other great spiritual teachers and leaders
of mankind! They gave of themselves completely to others so
that the world and all its inhabitants might reach something of
the stature of God, Who is present in the spirit of the soul, as
well as transcendent above all categories of thought. If we study
the lives of the great lovers of mankind—and Christ stands beyond the remainder in His redeeming function of all mankind—
we will see that their love set men free. They were freed from
the attraction of all subsidiary things, and could realise themselves as sons of God.

True love is concerned with the growing into maturity of the
beloved, who in the fullness of time includes all mankind and all
created things. It has that detached commitment to the person
at hand which supports him to the utmost while leaving him free
to be himself. In this way love makes no demands, neither does
it look for results. It is unaware of itself in its concern for the

other, and its recompense is helping the beloved to be more fully himself. It knows that all will be well in accordance with the will of God, and that its own function is to support and strengthen the beloved during the period of darkness and suffering.

Love in action
This does not mean that love separates itself purposely from other people. On the contrary, it knows when to be near, even intimate, for in union there is joy. When lovers are giving fully of themselves to and for each other, the Holy Spirit is working in them and between them, showing them the divine nature as they consummate their union. But there is also a time when the lovers must separate to fulfil their individual destinies, and in this conscious withdrawal the strength of caring and love is even stronger than when the lovers were together.

The two most powerful sentences of love come from St. John's gospel. In the third chapter (verses 27 to 36), St. John the Baptist speaks of his own eclipse as the power of Jesus grows: "He must increase, but I must decrease." This is love in action, that one may give all one has to help another and be diminished as the result of it. But the diminution is only in the world's eyes. It is a humbling that leads one to the divine. In the fifteenth chapter of the same gospel Jesus says, "Greater love hath no man than this, that a man lay down his life for his friends." Here the decrease moves to a complete surrender of the earthly personality, but once again the soul, which is the agent of real love, lies revealed, radiant, and triumphant.

In this understanding of true love we can glimpse a mature human relationship with God. He reveals Himself to us in mystical union, and we see His glory that surpasses all categories. Then we come down to the world once more, and the divine radiance is only a memory. We have to work on without the awareness of His constant presence, but as we progress to greater humanity, we realise that He is the power that is moving us onwards to the measure of perfection. In this way we may in the fullness of time be ever aware of Him, in no matter what circumstance we find ourselves.

In such a relationship of man and God there can be no turning back or loss of faith, for we know Him as He is and do not need to prove Him by signs and wonders. It is in this demand for a divine revelation that we tempt God. It is wise therefore to ponder on the most inscrutable clause of the Lord's prayer: "Lead us not into temptation", or as it is translated in the contemporary idiom, "do not bring us to the test". Of course, every episode of life is a test and a trial of our own endurance and faith. Without constant trials there would be no growth into the fullness of being. But we must work in faith based on the intuitive knowledge that God reveals to us. In so doing we will prevail against the darkness and transmute it into light. If, however, we challenge God's providence and power by demanding a "miracle", we will be left bereft of God's grace until we have learnt the error of our ways.

The test that we may dread is one of such magnitude that it challenges the very stuff of our being; it is right that we should not be brought to this test until we are so united in God that nothing can prevail against us. And who in this life do we know to be of such spiritual radiance? The diabolical techniques of torture and brain-washing that have been perfected in our own ultra-civilised generation have shown how few people, even those steeped in a religious tradition, are able to withstand psychological disintegration under such circumstances. It also shows us how few people have experienced the centre of their own being, for it is here alone, with God as ruler, that we stand impregnable against the assaults of the outer world. Religion and all its associations can actually separate us from the Spirit within, if we put our trust in these outer things instead of using them as a gateway to the inner life of the spirit.

Mature love is therefore not an emotional response; it is a quiet contemplation in which the whole being of the lover is centred on the being of the beloved. It is a state of union which grows in intensity until the lover and beloved are one in eternity. And when this happens every other creature is brought into union with them. Thus love never separates groups of people, but rather gathers them into a divine community that is the material, as well as mystical, Body of Christ. No one can ever love until he knows the love of God and can reciprocate that love with God. When the love is known, he can grow deeper in love with every created thing, seeing it, with all its blemishes, as a child of God.

This does not mean that love blinds itself to darkness and evil; on the contrary, it acknowledges them with unsentimental discernment. But it is no longer repelled by them. It descends to their level and raises them up to its own level. Thus is the darkness overcome by light, and the evil transmuted to good. The ministry of Christ showed this transfiguring process to perfection. His penetrating love changed all who came in contact with it, as it does even today. But there are many who cannot bear the implications of this discernment. They prefer to live in the darkness of their own illusions rather than be cleansed by the light of God. Thus they seek to destroy the healing light that emanates from love, but it cannot be overcome, for it is of the nature of God Himself.

Nevertheless, we come to know the love of God by actively dedicating ourselves to the world around us. Even the romantic love of youth is a gateway to the divine. But it is the frustration, the disappointment, of this personal attraction that first makes many people open to the unfailing love of God. He comes to us when we are broken, and He mends the personality within us. The gratitude we evince and the depth of understanding with which we are now endowed help us to feel into the sufferings of others. Thus does compassion develop.

It is an important landmark on the road of love to feel compassion with others, for now one is in real communication with them. When our compassion for the afflicted of this earth reaches such intensity that we berate God for this universal suffering, He comes to us and shows us another way besides that of world service. He teaches us to pray.

CHAPTER 6

Love and human relationships

"THOU SHALT LOVE THY neighbour as thyself" is the second great commandment. The mystic would expand this by adding, "because he is yourself". But such love requires great experience and is the real testing-ground of the spiritual life. Love is, above all, honest. Therefore you cannot start a relationship by blinding yourself to the defects in the other person. The tendency of some well-meaning people to ignore the dark side that is in all of us and to concentrate on the divinity that they feel is present in everyone is laudable in intention but fallacious in practice. It may lead to a condescending attitude of tolerance, but it does not bring about any true relationship with the person, by which both are healed. We must start by facing the reality that confronts us without judging, but at least accepting that all is not well.

This awareness is once again the mode of action towards spiritual enlightenment. The more aware we are of the difficulties present in another person, the more the inner searchlight illuminates our own shortcomings. It is a well-known axiom that we most dislike in others those defects that are part of our own burden. Thus a period of candid introspection should be the sequel of a feeling of antipathy towards someone else. This is far more constructive than scolding yourself for your lack of charity, an attitude that has undertones of condescension. Once again the principle is seen: face the facts of life, including your own deficiencies, with a calm appraisal and not an emotional outburst. Nothing is, in the final analysis, either irremediable or perfect. We work from the first polarity to the second; this is the most we can do. Detached commitment is the foundation on which to build our relationship, and this can never be cemented except by years of hard work and dedication of the self.

In relationships there are some people whom we instinctively like. There seems to be a pre-ordained harmony between us, and we flourish in each other's company. If this affinity were to be analysed it might be found to depend on minor mannerisms, a certain lightness of touch or sense of humour, or else agreement on some intellectual or political proposition. It is not difficult to flow out from our depth to such people. Towards others we feel neutral, some we tolerate in polite silence, and a few we find unbearable. And yet we have to love them all without in any way demanding that they change their character to conform with our own wishes. We have to learn that love is not an emotional response or a feeling. It is a state of willed tranquillity in which we can absorb the personality of the other individual and give of our very being to him. Indeed, we can do none of this on our own, but depend on the Holy Spirit to lighten our soul with love, which comes to us as a revelation of the greater meaning of the life of the person against whom we may be fighting.

To start to love anyone, whether someone we already like or someone we actively dislike, requires a combination of silent attentiveness to him and prayer to God. In this attention we give of ourselves to the person and listen to him. What he has to say or what mood he emanates speaks to our own condition, telling us about the state of our own life. And this attention culminates in a response, which must be both definite and honest. In the early stages of a relationship much unpleasant psychological material from the unconscious is released, and we have to learn to assimilate it. We may betray our own ideals of calmness and politeness in a heated exchange, but however humiliated we may feel, we are at least being led to the truth about ourselves, and are really relating to the other person. Bland politeness is often a negation of relationships.

The constructive role of conflict in the establishment of harmony is not fully appreciated. The importance of conflict is that it lays the soul bare and also reveals to the light of reason the dark elements of the unconscious that usually obscure the soul. Relationship means willed attention to another person and a positive response to him. This response may be conventional and polite in neutral circumstances, but when the question of moral values arises, truth triumphs over politeness. It is not at all bad that in the early stages hard words and hurt feelings should abound. The very break in psychic communion is an important landmark in a relationship, for it teaches one in a negative way the wrong approach to another person and the deep need one has for real harmony. This harmony is not one of uniformity of belief or practice. It is a harmony of mature people who can be themselves without embarrassment or apology in the company of others. Peace at the price of betraying one's own deepest convictions may be necessary in certain circumstances, but it has nothing of harmony in it. At the very best it is a makeshift compromise, and the equilibrium maintained is an uneasy one.

Yet many, and probably most, relationships are of this order. It is uncommon to find husband and wife relating to each other in such a way that each is completely free and realising his (or her) full potentialities as a person. It is much more frequent for one to submerge the drive for growth in order to accommodate the other. The same applies in the family where there is tension between parents and children, or in working life where there is disharmony between different grades of employees or between employer and employee.

None of this is necessarily bad, nor is the judgment all in favour of the one against the other. The sharp distinction between black and white is an attitude of immaturity. The purpose of living is to penetrate ever more deeply into the lives and characters of other people, not in order to judge or change them but to learn more about oneself. You learn half this lesson during periods of solitude when you are thrown back on your own resources, and the other half when you are responding to various assaults of the outside world, which in practice means confrontations with other people. And the final goal is to be able to love those people and the whole created universe around you.

The first step

The first step in loving is to be able to distinguish it from liking, which is, as already stated, a superficial emotional response. It is largely instinctive and it cannot be cultivated. But love is a life's work, and it requires the consecration of your whole being to achieve it. It is in fact impossible to love anyone with mature power until one is tractable to that love which

comes from outside. This is the love of God. But we can make
ourselves more receptive to that all-embracing love by discipline
in relationships.

The three actions needed in this discipline are *willed attention,*
honesty, and *quiet receptiveness.* The first is the intention to
listen and observe. Too much conversation is merely a means of
relieving ourselves of words and ideas, of speaking at rather than
to people. We have no real interest in what they feel or how
they are fulfilling their own lives. We are concerned only about
their reaction to us, to our ideas, and especially to our personality.
The number of people who can bear to remain silent and listen
is very small when compared with those who have to be in the
company of others and to be talking the whole time. And yet it
is the silent ones who are usually communicating at a far deeper
level of personality than those who are garrulous. Nothing separates people so completely as words and ideas, when they are
afraid to reveal themselves fully to others. To pay the other person the compliment of being interested in him and what he has
to say is the beginning of a real relationship with him. If one
can also be pleased to see him the relationship is flourishing, and
love is beginning to develop.

But there must be honesty. One cannot be pleased to see
everybody, at least in the early stages of the spiritual life. Therefore we must acknowledge our unease, and not try to diminish
it or explain it away. It is in the height of conflict that the truth
about ourselves and the other person becomes revealed. To
understand all is to forgive all, but it takes a long time before
complete understanding can be established. First you have to
gain deeper knowledge of the background of the other person,
and, secondly, you have to understand your own weaknesses that
are so devastatingly exposed in this relationship. All this is not
easy. In the spiritual life you are confronted by a psychoanalyst
who is your own soul guided by the Holy Spirit. When we are
most abject we are also most receptive to divine grace.

This brings us to the matter of quiet receptiveness. We can
never mend a relationship or start to love another person by our
own efforts alone. Something else has to be added. Even if we
have considerable insight into the cause and nature of the disharmony, we can never effect that change of heart that is the true
measure of inner healing. This change comes as a thief in the

night, when we least expect it, and it is wrought by persistent prayer.

It is this ability to submit to the inevitable and to God at the same time that brings love into the personality. And prayer is rendered in the quietness of the soul where we are most receptive to God. The first and last insight of the spiritual life is that we alone can do nothing, but that both within us and outside us there is a power ready to come to our aid if we but have the humility to invoke it. It is a manifestation of God once more, this time much less personal and much more transpersonal. By this I mean that the divine nature does not reveal itself to us as a personal relationship between God and the individual, but rather as an all-embracing power of love that cares for all its creatures infinitely. It moves beyond the narrow confines of personality to reveal a unity that contains all created things within it, and transcends the sum of these creatures. This revelation of divine grace is an even more perfect meeting with God than an early conversion experience in which He speaks directly to the soul. A relationship of this latter type is rather exclusive, whereas an experience that brings in all created things ends not in exclusive claims but in an all-embracing love. When we throw ourselves open to divine grace it is the soul that is laid bare. Once the soul is experienced, its intimate communication with all other souls is realised, and a mystical awareness of the soul of all mankind in communion with Christ dawns on the observer. In such awareness, personality (including personal antipathy) is included in the larger communion of men, which is the mystical body of Christ, and enmity against a particular person simply ceases to exist. Instead, loving care develops.

The act of forgiveness is one that is given to us by God. We can never by our own will forgive with that complete change of heart which is the proof of real forgiveness. And as we surrender ourselves to forgive others, so we ourselves are forgiven. The proof of this change in heart of which I speak is a changed attitude not only to the person who has been forgiven, but also to the meaning of our own lives. Once we know of the forgiveness of God to another person so we begin to guard our own inner domain of personality with less anxiety. We become less concerned about our reputation, about the danger of betrayal by others, about the sincerity of the one whom we have forgiven. Indeed, the episodes of the past that caused the disharmony fade into insignificance and eventually into oblivion when compared with the radiance of God's love in the soul. He who knows God in the height of his being no longer needs the propitiation and approbation of men. Instead he has their love, for he no longer demands it but rather flows out in love to them. It may take years of patient endeavour in constant prayer to reach this state of unconditional forgiveness, but when it is attained, we are changed. We have known God face to face. A new view of reality is cleared in front of us.

What a difference there is between this growth into harmony and an attitude of mind that refuses to face the fact of disharmony in the first place and merely plasters a broken relationship with platitudes and clichés! There are unfortunately some relationships that will not be healed in this lifetime. It may be because of the absolute intransigence of the other person; it may be a symptom of severe mental illness. This type of difficulty is seen repeatedly in marital relationships when there is a fundamental incompatibility between the two partners, and it also blights the working lives of many employees and employers. Once again there is no magical solution to the difficulty. To break connexion at once is not the answer. It is right that we should persevere in faith for an amelioration of the discord. Often a completely unexpected event, such as a communal tragedy, shows the difficult person in a new light, and quite unsuspected kindness and consideration flow from him. We should never despair of anyone, nor should we exalt another person too highly. We all have feet of clay in certain circumstances, and we all show the undistorted image of God that lies in the soul on other occasions. The more we grow in spiritual depth, the more repeatedly are we put to shame by the kindness, loyalty, and patience of people who are dismissed as being of no account by the world at large. And who knows when Christ may reveal Himself once more in the cleaner, the labourer, or the garage attendant! He is much more likely to appear in such a guise than in that of the distinguished professor, auspicious prelate, or powerful magnate. These latter are all too often so aware of themselves and their important role in society that they have no contact with the unseen world at all.

This does not mean that a spiritual man suffers in silence under abuse. Not only is this a denial of relationships but it also does nothing to help the abuser, who is in great need of healing.

A positive response, even if threatening and hostile, at least clears the air so that honesty can prevail. If the abuse continues, it may well be necessary to fight the unbalanced person until he comes to his senses. Honest conflict reveals depths in all the combatants and helps them to meet one another with respect. It is thus that love develops. There are also times when it is right to turn the other cheek and put up no resistance. This is especially so when one is attacked by obviously deranged, unhappy people. What they need is loving care so that they may cease to fight society for its indifference to them. The important thing in any difficult situation of this type is that one should detach oneself from the anger of wounded pride. This can be done only by praying to God for help and support during the heat of the encounter. In this way one is spared adding to the unhappiness by saying unpleasant things or behaving in a wounded, sulky fashion.

It is this type of forbearance that is at the heart of the injunctions against violence in the Sermon on the Mount. If we wait on God, His Spirit will guide us into the truth of the situation and tell us when to respond with positive action and when to submit in charity. For too much discord is based on the desire for personal justification. As we grow in the spiritual life we need to justify and excuse ourselves much less than before, for we are more in control of ourselves and can act more in acceptance with the divine will. Thus we are more able to lose our lives in love for others.

Not every difficult relationship will be mended in this lifetime. In that case circumstances will conspire to move us away from the focus of trouble, but only after we have learned our lesson well. This lesson has two parts: the reason why we are involved in the first place, and the strength that has been gained as a result of the trial. When we are freed, we should come out as stronger, more alive people, less likely to make the same mistakes a second time. But if we move away at the slightest intimation of trouble, we cannot grow into mature human beings. One unfortunate relationship will follow another, and we will never come to understand the weakness in our own character. Only by confronting the difficulty here and now can we reach true understanding. We may emerge battered and bruised, but at least we now know where we stand. Our very wounds will be made worships, as Dame Julian of Norwich was shown. The one glorious result of prevailing over a personal tragedy is that our perspectives enlarge, and we realise how trivial were many of the things that we had previously considered essential to our happiness.

Depth in relationships

While the spiritual life leads to an increasing depth of communication with many different types of people, there is also a place in it for the uniquely deep relationship of marriage. The marriage relationship should be a stable union between two people who are growing into maturity together. This growth is both physical and spiritual. Neither aspect is complete without the other. The pendulum has swung far from the traditional position that the physical part of sex, though inevitable, is best dismissed as soon as possible so that the spiritual side of marriage can be extolled without shame. Of course, this division of anything in the world into "physical" and "spiritual" is fallacious. The incarnate Christ speaks, as no other religious figure in the world's history does, of the glory and holiness of matter, a tradition that is part of the Judaic heritage of which He partook. The physical part of sex is a sacrament, and it is dishonoured only to the shame of those who corrupt it. But if the sexual act is to be consummated in holiness, there must be real love between the two partners. Admittedly the concept of love deepens in sublimity as we grow older in the spiritual life, but the caring of the one for the other should be present from the start of the relationship.

It is unfortunate that the pendulum has now swung so far towards the side of physical gratification that the emotional and spiritual results of sexual union are seldom given their due. Thus sex has to a great extent been separated, even divorced, from love. It has been reduced to a pleasurable physiological act whose performance is helpful psychologically! From this attitude develops promiscuity and an animal-like attitude to the welfare of other people. In short, thoughtless sexual gratification leads to ever increasing selfishness. The other person becomes a mere chattel for satisfaction, and when this person is a woman and she is discarded, there is often a festering wound left behind. The view is widely current in some quarters that permanent marriage is a bad, if not impossible, state of affairs, and that men (less often women, interestingly enough) should be allowed variety in their sexual life once they become bored with their present partner. Understandable as this may be on a biological level, it is not conducive to the growth of the person to full maturity. There is no real personal relationship in such a life, only a succession of selfish liaisons. True concern for another person cannot use sex in this selfish way. Sexual union is, on the contrary, a manifestation of the deepest regard that one human being has for another. And the sexual part of marriage, vital as it is in most instances, is only one aspect of a loving relationship. It is the growth of both partners into the love of God, where there is complete liberty, that is the true end of marriage.

Celibacy

Celibacy is to be seen in this light. It is the path of the few who are so filled with love that their concern is for God in all His works, and therefore with all mankind. Instead of devoting his attention to one particular person (and the family that may arise), the celibate is involved in all the world's tragedy, and his work is giving himself to be a living sacrifice for many people. This is the life of Christ. It is not to be exalted above the married state, for both are ways of life that lead to God. But it must be understood that the celibate life is not an escape from deep commitment to another person. It is a giving of one's whole self to the world. It is a state of the liberty that comes from the Holy Spirit, but it has little worldly comfort to enjoy.

"I must be about my Father's business" is the watchword of the celibate life. No one should take that way until he knows his motives well. It is the harder path, but its prize is all the more worth while. This celibate life is sometimes also the completion of married life when one of the partners has died. It is then that the love of man is extended through a love of all men to the threshold of God. In Him all are united, the living and the dead, in eternity.

I have touched on the role of suffering in spiritual development. Now we must look at this in much greater depth, for it is profoundly relevant to the growth of the spiritual life.

CHAPTER 7

The role of suffering

LIVING IS NOT A STATIC process, it is one of constant movement. The upheaval of past assumptions is part of the travail of growth. As we collect ourselves, battered and torn, from a present calamity, so we are able to discern more clearly what is really important and what is mere dross. Suffering is an inevitable part of the growth into the spiritual life. Without it we would remain in that dormant position that is real death. As we saw earlier, many people come to a knowledge of God through suffering; when they are bereft of all human sustenance, they are at last receptive to divine grace. But suffering continues after the awareness of God touches the soul. It is with us until the end of created life.

Let it be said at once that there is no completely satisfactory explanation of suffering in the face of the all-powerful, all-loving God of theism. It is wisest to start with the assumption that when He made them, He gave His creatures (which means especially man, at least in relation to the world we inhabit) such free will that they could, in the fullness of time and when they were mature individuals, return to Him voluntarily, not as coerced slaves but as free agents. It is man's destiny to work with the living God to create a world of such beauty and harmony that it may be raised to spiritual stature. But free will is a double-edged sword: it is almost always used first for self-aggrandisement, and only when the fruits of this are experienced does the will work on a wider, more altruistic basis. There is much in the world's disharmony that is due to the selfish, "fallen" condition of nature, and especially of man. It could be that even such natural disasters as earthquakes, floods, and famine are due to the wrong actions and attitudes of the world's inhabitants, especially human beings.

Such a view of suffering has at least the merit of seeing its constructive role in the evolution of man, without in any way trying to minimise its effects or dismiss it as an illusion due to man's wrong thinking. Since there is one God, and all are embraced in Him and infused by Him, it follows that the darkness and evil of the world are as much a part of the divine providence as is that which appears good and radiant to us. Indeed, such duality lies more in the minds of immature people than in reality. The mystic is given a glimpse of a divine unity that comprehends and reconciles darkness and light in such a way that there is a synthesis in which both are combined and transfigured into a new light of spiritual radiance. This is the uncreated light that is seen in mystical illumination, and will be discussed later.

It is amusing to listen to professed atheists denying the existence of God because of the terrible sufferings and injustices in the world. Yet their very indignation, so praiseworthy in its compassion for all suffering beings, speaks of an intuitive knowledge of God that lies deep in their own souls, a knowledge whose promise is betrayed by the actions of their fellow men and the inscrutable workings of the cosmic law. Our very intimation of perfection, of how things ought to happen, is the voice of God within us. It is no use raging against the world and its corruption. We have to be like Isaiah, who after his mystical vision in the temple was filled with an awareness of his own sinfulness. When this was removed, he could say to God, "Here am I; send me."

Suffering is the reaction of a static body or mind to the onward flow of life. It tells us that our present attitudes and responses, adequate as they may have been at a previous period of our lives, are no longer enough. As we move into the spirit of truth we are called on to relinquish more and more of the possessions, the impediments, that we once thought were essential for our well-being. This does not mean that we are called on to sacrifice everything either at once or even finally. It means that, as I emphasised earlier, we must have a completely changed attitude to possessions so that we are no longer enslaved by them. It is a joyful thought that suffering is the way to liberation, and that every unpleasant circumstance, if endured with awareness and acceptance, hastens our growth into spiritual reality.

Suffering takes many forms. The most simple are related to the loss of material and emotional benefits. The most terrible is the fear that you have slipped from divine grace, because you can no longer feel a communication with God. This is "the dark night of the soul" that is so well known by mystics in their ascent to the mountain of transfiguration. When we dedicate ourselves to the service of God, our motives are tested very agonisingly. It is one thing to accept God in His personal revelation to us, but quite another to work under the person of God until our souls respond perfectly to His will. This is the spiritual path. Many people believe that the path to God is one of radiance, of peace, and of health; that as we put aside the old forms of thinking and put God mentally in charge of our lives, so He leads us into greater happiness and prosperity. Indeed, they believe that if our lives are not progressing with such success, there must be something wrong with our attitude. This is the type of glib assumption made by many popular schools of "positive thinking". As in so many other instances, this point of view is neither completely wrong nor is it the whole truth. There can be no doubt that the path to God is the one to success in worldly living also, but the measure of this success is often very different from that envisaged by the naïve, optimistic theist. Since we have to lose our very personality in order to discover the soul within it, it follows that the divine path is one littered with many past illusions, some of which may have been very dear to us in an earlier part of our life.

When we consecrate our souls to God, He tests them in the purifying fire of experience. It is very often that the aspirant, after his first glimpse of God, is cast down in the mire of tragedy. All the stable connexions from which he previously drew strength are withdrawn, and even his health may fail. The radiant light that drew him towards the greater world of reality dims, and all that is left is his own faith. This is the test of sincerity in the spiritual path, that we persist in our dedication to God when He appears to withdraw all his visible comforts from us. And do not imagine that this dark night of the soul, when all around us is the mist of obscurity, is merely an evanescent phase. It may go on indefinitely, or it may be punctuated by brief phases of bliss that are, in their turn, enveloped in a greater darkness. The measure of this darkness is the inability of the intellect to penetrate it. It is a void of blackness, and it is devoid even of emotional content.

In some instances the darkness can be related to unfavourable outer circumstances such as marital disharmony, ill health, or financial difficulties. But these are largely coincidental. It is tempting to blame one's inner dereliction on outer difficulties, but in fact these merely provide an excuse for leaving the great quest. We have to penetrate far deeper than the trivialities of worldly living if we are to transcend the darkness of the soul. There is, however, one bright spark of hope that remains during the test of aptitude, and this is a dim realisation of the fact that we have moved from the world of triviality and social usage to a numinous realm of unseen potentiality. What it embraces we cannot directly know at this stage, but in an inscrutable way it harmonises with the pulse of faith that is the inner manifestation of the soul's action. In other words, it is impossible to go back to where we were before the call to God inflamed the soul. If there is a great temptation to relapse to old ways and ends, the call has been spurious, and one has to retrace one's steps very carefully. But this state of affairs is unknown to those dedicated to the search for true life. The very darkness is a rest to the weary mind, and in it our earthly desires can find a welcome oblivion.

Divine reality

The most disturbing feature of this darkness is the soul's apparent inability to reach the divine presence by any mental action. Articulated prayer and the ritual imagery of religious worship cease to engage the heart. Books of devotion and even the scriptures themselves fall on deaf ears. The outer suffering that may be a coincidental part of the state of darkness goes on unabated, and such prayer as the aspirant can offer has no ameliorative effect. The friends and advisers of the aspirant are usually of little help unless they are people of real spiritual experience. Indeed, the modern leaning towards psychotherapy can be a snare when it is deflected towards the spiritual life. It is easy for an agnostic psychotherapist to attribute spiritual darkness to a morbid depressive state, due either to an endogenous dysfunction of the brain or else to unfulfilled sexual or secular ambitions. But the proof of the inadequacy of this type of approach is the sharp sanity of the aspirant and his hidden will to progress to a new life. The panaceas of the liberal worldly society, such as material affluence, sexual satisfaction, and personal gratification, are seen by him to be inadequate for the new dimension of life that has opened up before him. Indeed, there is no one steeped in worldly thought who can help the suffering spiritual seeker; his help comes directly from the spirit in his soul, where God is immanent.

The truth is that a new understanding of divine reality is being given to the aspirant. God is so far beyond mortal conception that He is known to the mind as infinite darkness. Whatever pictures, views, or concepts of God we may cherish in our day-to-day lives are completely overshadowed by the divine radiance, which by its very light blinds our intellectual faculties. This does not imply that God is opposed to the reasoning mind, or that He has nothing to impart to the intellectual aspect of personality. He can, however, never be traced and circumscribed according to man's reason. Reason can never penetrate as far as God, but God can infuse the reasoning faculty by a downpouring of light that is known as enlightenment to the intellectual function of the personality. Thus as our material, emotional, and rational conceits are lifted progressively from us by the purifying fire of suffering, so we come to see God less and less as a circumscribed Person and more as the totality of being.

The mystics describe Him as that which is. The more we are like Him the more we are in our own essence, and the less do we have to assert ourselves.

A growth into God is a growth away from submergence in the sufferings germane to one's own life or even of the world as a whole. This does not mean that we are lifted out of situations of suffering by a magical technique (some current schools of thought describe their practitioners as being "above" the pain of the world, though in fact an acquaintance with these people soon shows their personal inadequacy). The acceptance of suffering, neither in supine resignation nor in rebellious antipathy, is the measure of one's growth into God. If our proof of God depends on His success in alleviating pain and promoting worldly success, we know little of Him. We are, in fact, more likely to be in contact with suspect lower forces. The real evidence of God is the ability of the soul to rest in Him, no matter how terrible the outer circumstances appear. He is the darkness of the intellect and the dullness of the emotions, but He is also the light of the soul. When He is seen, the mind and emotions are still, quiet, and at rest, for a new organ of perception acclaims Him. The soul is revealed in its glory, and its organs of apprehension are active.

As the new revelation of divine grace is accepted and understood, so there is a subtle change in our consciousness, and a new way of life opens. The suffering of the present time, to use St. Paul's expression, is not to be compared with the glory that is to be revealed in us—and is being revealed every day as we move fearlessly into the unknown yet foreseen danger, not counting the cost but dedicating everything we have to Him Who gives us everything. If the farewell discourses of Jesus, written in the fourteenth to the seventeenth chapters of the Gospel according to St. John, are read in the light of His suffering on the cross, such suffering is seen to be the inevitable precursor of glorification. There is no glorification of the personality so that it is transfigured by the light of God, except through the refining fire of suffering.

The suffering that leads the soul to a heightened awareness of God is a part of the journey of the person to the light. This suffering is never actively sought nor is it exulted over. It has little relationship with the self-induced suffering that follows a selfish, ignorant, or reckless action. Such suffering, which is an inevitable sequel to a wrong action, may also lead one to a greater understanding of God's grace if one accepts it as a new adventure in living. But this type of travail is at the foot-hills of the mountain of transfiguration. It is only the start of the spiritual ascent, and its consummation is that experience of forgiveness that has already been touched on in connexion with love. The suffering that is part of the spiritual life itself is an immersion of the soul into the darkness of the world, where it feels in its very core the hopelessness and dereliction of unredeemed mankind—and indeed all created things. These are all striving, even in their ignorance, for the inner perfection that is the person's intuitive knowledge of God, but they do not know where they are going. Yet even in the darkness of their ignorance God is in control, and He will lead them to enlightenment. It is the service of the aspirant, in partaking of this darkness and even in being one with it, to lead benighted mankind out of its isolated ignorance into the greater community of God. In the world's history it was the incarnate Christ who performed this function in His own

time, and through the power of the Holy Spirit He continues
in the lives of all those, of every religious denomination and of
none, who dedicate themselves to the loving service of their
fellow-men. These are the real Christians, whether or not they
accept the name.

Any superficial approach to suffering which looks for its root
in a wrong action in the past is quite inadequate. The most spiritual people it has been my privilege to know have had hard lives
punctuated by much personal tribulation. And in every case this
suffering, by being accepted, has raised them to that glory that
was seen fully in the resurrected Christ.

I will now outline the history of three such people.

CHAPTER 8

Strength in weakness

MY FIRST FRIEND CAME from a rather conventional Christian background, against which he revolted early in his life. The narrowness of its theology appalled him, for he was a universalist at heart. He could not accept the traditional image of a personal God who could be bribed and placated by eloquent prayers, and had special regard for those whose theology was right. For many years he was a seeking, reverent agnostic. He was a scientist by training with special knowledge of chemistry and biology, and he worked with a well-known firm of industrial chemists for many years. His work took him to many places and countries, and the starvation he saw in vast areas of the world filled him with indignation. A man of innate compassion, he grieved over the world's sufferings and dedicated himself to the relief of world hunger, a concern that remained with him to the time of his death.

He had once to visit Tibet during his duties in China, a country that fascinated him. One night as he strolled by the shores of a beautiful lake overshadowed by high mountain peaks, a stillness came over him. The peace of God touched his soul, and he was at last given the directive that his life had previously been awaiting. He dedicated himself at that very moment to God's service, offering himself unconditionally to mankind. Then he left the Far East and returned home.

At once disaster struck. His wife, with whom he had never had a real relationship, fell ill, and she grew progressively more estranged from him. His children followed their mother's way. His finances failed soon afterwards, and he became chronically ill for many years. Yet despite the collapse of his private life, he dedicated himself to the service of others. He had a remarkable healing gift, and he spent his time travelling all over the country giving spiritual healing, counsel, and solace to all who called upon him. He never charged any money for his services, even travelling on his own account. Much of his time was occupied in helping agnostics to accept a meaning for their sufferings, and to believe that human personality does survive the death of the physical body. (It should be noted that not a few of these spiritual agnostics were devoted churchgoers, whose religion unfortunately had not penetrated beneath the surface of their personalities.)

In his work he was helped devotedly by his second wife, and their combined ministry was a source of inspiration to all who knew them. And yet there was never a real release from physical suffering despite his great work of healing others.

When I first met him he was nearly eighty years old and his youthfulness was a constant delight. Like all really young people (who are in fact ageless) he kept his youthfulness by interesting himself in every current trend in science, philosophy, and theology. But when he was in his middle eighties he was struck down with cancer. His body could not stand this fresh blow, and the radical treatment necessary for this grave disease produced a profound mental depression. He rallied outwardly, but the soul was slowly being released from the ailing body. His sufferings were much more spiritual than physical, and he died six months after his disease became manifest. This was not the manner of death that his friends had envisaged. But then was not the Christ crucified between two criminals while the mob jeered at Him for His manifest helplessness?

How little the naked eye sees if it is not filled with celestial vision.

My second friend, also elderly when I knew him, was distinguished by a most brilliant mind. He belonged to the now almost extinct class of highly educated people whose minds could embrace the whole breadth of European culture and philosophy, and also understand the nuances of Eastern religious thought. He was an intellectual, a highly successful man of business, a great student of Jungian psychology, and a near mystic. To be in his company was a great intellectual experience, but he could be cruel to those of lesser mental ability and selfish in his personal relationships. All this contrasted painfully with the fluent wisdom that emanated from his mind. To suffer fools gladly is a difficult task, but until it is accomplished, you are not a whole person—for God is nearer to the fool than to the intellectual!

About a year before his death, he was stricken by a severe heart attack. Indeed, he should have died at one point, but was brought round by expert resuscitation. The experience of passing over was important for him, because he had already become interested in the fate of the psyche of those whose bodies had died. His first response to the new lease of life granted him was blissful, but soon it was succeeded by a most terrible depression which lasted a number of months. During this period he repudiated and betrayed every spiritual principle that had previously sustained his life and that he had inculcated into those who had had the privilege of being his students. A nihilistic despair dominated his conscious life, and he was cynically suspicious of those around him who loved him dearly.

As the months passed, this terrible despair gradually lifted, and the last time I saw him he was markedly euphoric, being filled with grandiose schemes for the future, but also harbouring suspicion of those around him. He gradually returned to his old self, but was now much quieter and more rested than previously. He began to cling with real affection to his saintly wife who had sustained his work over the years despite frequent ingratitude. As the new year came in he acknowledged the primacy of love above all else in life. Of course, he knew this with the mind—the reason or the intellect—well enough before the final testing. But at last it had penetrated through the heart to the soul. And he was redeemed.

He was in fact planning new work when a second heart attack struck, and he died almost immediately.

My third friend, to whom I owe more than I could ever say, was a woman who was a natural mystic. Brought up in a conventional, but not unpleasant, Christian background, she too showed an early universalism which transcended narrow denominational barriers. After disillusionment during the first world war, she drifted aimlessly along for a time, but always with an inner directive to find out the meaning that lay behind the strange façade of outer life. From war nursing she moved into the new field of family planning and from there into a uniquely practical type of psychology that acknowledged the soul as the primary unit of man's being. Of course, this view is, in one respect, as old as mankind, but, on the other hand, it has been almost entirely overlaid with more materialistic psychological theories that deride all assertions of spirituality as wishful thinking.

My friend had no doubt that the great fact of psychology was that man was a spiritual being. But as she lacked those degrees and diplomas that the world looks for as a gauge of respectability, she was always an outsider. Nevertheless, her classes were extremely well attended in the earlier part of her work, and many people in all walks of life benefited from her sound teaching and spiritual counsel. Many took from her but few paid her the courtesy of acknowledging the source of their wisdom. But her generosity was such that her only wish was that her teaching should be as widely disseminated as possible so as to give new hope and inspiration to those cast down and in trouble.

As she grew older the sunniness of her disposition dulled and she became increasingly petulant and irritable. She felt she had failed in her work, for her classes were becoming very poorly attended. Life was passing her by despite her great gifts and her spiritual vision. Indeed, towards the end of her active life one became wary of meeting her. It was indeed sad to behold a person who had given of herself, body and soul, to her vocation become bitter with the passage of years. She ate too much, more through frustration than greed, and her blood pressure rose dangerously. Finally she had a severe stroke.

For over two years she remained alive, completely paralysed down the right side of her body and virtually speechless. All she could utter were a few meaningless words, and direct communication with her was more through loving intuition than by words of intelligence. Yet those two years were the crowning glory of this great woman's life, because what she had taught about the soul was now radiating through her own being. Being bereft of intellectual conceit and physical pride, she had nothing else but the light from within, and how radiantly this shone. She became a focus of benediction for the entire geriatric hospital where she spent this last period of her life. She had become as a little child who alone can enter the kingdom of God. The nurses, sensible practical women far too accustomed to the squalid facts of chronic illness to indulge in sentimental make-believe, flowed out in love to this speechless, yet strangely articulate, soul. They brought other patients to her, so that by holding her hand, they could obtain a blessing. A distinguished neurologist who was called in to see her and advise about the possibility of further treatment, while having nothing further to contribute in this matter, remarked on the splendid personality that must once have been present despite the tragic disintegration that was now taking place. Indeed, this last period was a blessing, and to be in her presence was an experience of divine grace.

When she was finally carried off by a second stroke there was great sadness among the patients and staff. She could not communicate with words, but her soul established that deeper communication which is the heart of real communion. When the claims of the rebellious personality were finally stilled, the soul shone through directly, and she took all those round her to the threshold of the divine presence.

Prolonged test

It would be an anticlimax to expatiate on the crowning strength that came with weakness in the life histories of my three friends. But I should not fail to point out one consideration. All had to undergo a prolonged test of physical disease before they were relieved by death. Had their lives not been prolonged they could not have worked out what they came into the world to achieve.

There is a temptation nowadays to advocate a modified euthanasia of those who are incurably ill. While I do not wish to make, from these instances of redemption by suffering, a dogma in favour of prolonging the lives of those whose existence seems to have lost all meaning, I would counsel the utmost caution against glib assumptions about the quality of any particular life. *We do not know what lessons the soul is learning while the person lies in the deepest humiliation.* If we knew more about eternal life, we would live our present life-span on earth with greater reverence and joy.

The mind is extremely humbled by the radiance of soul made manifest in those who suffer. Of course, not all victims of strokes emanate love as did my friend. Many become selfish, querulous, and destructive. But even in this there may be a lesson. The soul might be learning through the disintegration of the superficial personality, which had previously successfully hidden its inner darkness behind a veneer of piety. When the meretricious surface is removed, its inner depths are revealed, and what emanates is not pleasant. But we must stop judging, and observe the travail of the soul with detached compassion. It is thus that judgment is transcended by understanding, and a vaster view of the process of life in eternity becomes visible to us.

With these considerations behind us, we are now ready to look more deeply at the inner life.

CHAPTER 9

The inner life

THERE IS A PORTION of our life that has to be spent in solitude. Indeed, in one respect we are always in solitude, for no human being can fully penetrate the depths of feeling of another person's life. Thus the two most important events in anyone's life—his birth and his death—are always solitary even though their external circumstances may be attended by a number of people. The experience of loneliness is a very necessary episode on the road to divine recognition, for it is in God alone that we can effect a true relationship which is constant and sustaining. Thus the life of solitude is the life that leads to the direct experience of God, in whom alone we can find that rest that is truly dynamic activity. "He who has the Son has life," says St. John. He who knows the Son within himself is in harmony with all conditions of men. His solitude is consummated in that relationship which brings into reality the communion of saints.

The inner life is one in which we penetrate the depth of our own natural isolation in order to attain to a knowledge of the power that sustains us, the power of God. When you are naturally shy and find you cannot mix with other people on the superficial level of pleasantry that passes for friendship in most societies, you should not be unnecessarily worried about this isolation. You are being given the opportunity to penetrate beneath sociability to a real depth of life. You will never make friends by forcing yourself to be with people, by joining clubs and societies that do not really interest you, or even by making yourself useful to others on a charitable basis. You have first to learn to know yourself and to accept yourself as you are, without in any way blinding yourself to your many defects. It is only when we are at one with ourselves as we now stand that we can flow out to others in unreserved attention and concern. This is the inner part of loving. We cannot even ask God to help us love another person until we have learnt to accept ourselves, even indeed to love ourselves, as we now stand. And this self-love is again a divine gift.

To speak of loving yourself sounds very heretical to the conventionally religious person who has learnt, through the repetition of confessional statements, to see himself as a miserable sinner in whom there is no good at all. The traditional theology of the fall of man, inherited from Adam's fatal error, sees human nature as totally corrupt. It is one of the more fortunate results of modern scientific understanding, based on the theory of evolution and modern depth psychology, that this crude interpretation of the fall is now being superseded by a more enlightened view of human nature. Man is a spiritual being—by which I mean a person capable of conscious union with God through the action of a morally enlightened will—living in an animal body. And this body, transient as it is in terms of the immortality of the soul (which is the organ of the spirit), is a holy creation. Its impulses move it to survival and procreation, without which the soul would be impotent while on earth. The Hebraic insight about the fundamental unity of soul and body is the truth, and it stresses the fact that spirituality infuses every act of life, not only prayer and religious observances but also the work by which we earn our living, the sexual life whereby we grow in relationship and procreate, and the acts of eating and excreting whereby the body maintains its health. The joy of worldly life is the acme of spirituality, and no action is too mean to be beneath the influence of the Holy Spirit. Thus high spirits, a sense of fun, and an enjoyment of the physical beauty of the world (including other people) are all spiritual faculties that should be encouraged and not suppressed.

If an over-emphasis on the body (the common attitude in contemporary society) leads to a hedonistic view of life that ends in the meaninglessness of decrepitude and death, so also an over-emphasis on the soul leads to a life-denying flight from reality which is often confused with spirituality, but which in fact thwarts any growth of the personality. The soul grows through its restriction in matter during the process of incarnation. It is the growth in disciplined limitation that alone can lead to a union with God. Thus the body and its chthonic (earthy) instincts are good provided they are under the control of the soul. They become demonic when they take charge of the personality and lead the individual to a life of mere self-gratification.

To love yourself is to accept yourself as you are, and to thank God that you are as He made you. This does not mean self-inflation, as the Pharisee in the parable thanked God that he was not like other men such as the miserable publican. It means an open-hearted acceptance of our whole nature, the good and the bad, the radiant and the dark, without judgment, and a dedication of one's whole being, weak and defective though it may be, to God's service. The dark recesses of the personality are as much part of God's providence as the gifts and talents He has bestowed upon us. It requires no great effort to accept and glorify the fine aspects of our personality. It requires a lifetime of hard work and compassion to see that our defects are even more important portals to the divine grace. "My strength is made perfect in weakness." This does not mean that we should be sentimental about our weaknesses, excusing them conveniently as inevitable by-products of faulty education or heredity. It means that we must accept them directly, cease castigating ourselves over them, and begin to use them constructively in our lives.

The constructive use of a defect leads to greater compassion firstly towards other people with similar impediments and finally towards ourselves. We have a blue-print of perfection in our own souls; this blue-print is of God, who is the way to perfection as well as the perfection itself. We recognise perfection as that which leads us towards the ineffable Godhead. A perfect person (the incarnate Christ) or a perfect work of art is not one in which all positive attributes of truth, beauty, and goodness (or love) reach their final manifestation. Any such finality, while dazzling us for a period of time, would soon lead to boredom and decay. There is one end of perfection only, and that is union with God, Who transcends all categories of rational thought. Of Him nothing is known except through the experience of union that comes from love. Thus the perfection of which we are to partake is one that leads us beyond the exigent to the eternal, beyond the personal to the universal, beyond the temporal to the immortal. All great work, whether in science, art, or especially in human actions, leads us beyond finality to eternity.

It is our defects which, while they reveal how far we are from God, also show us the way to His grace. Our talents and gifts are the real snares that lie in the way of spiritual progress, and I am not speaking merely of such superficial gifts as physical beauty, intellectual brilliance, or artistic performance. These can quite clearly lead to self-inflation and pride. But it is the gifts of the spirit—which are largely psychic—that can very easily obscure our view of God. Anything that exalts the personality diminishes the soul. Anything that inspires the soul integrates the personality so that it becomes an ever more perfect vesture of the spirit. It is the awareness of our faults that illuminates the path to perfection. Once we have confessed our sins and acknowledged our deficiencies, we can in faith call for divine aid to lighten our inner darkness. Thus is the soul inspired. Great art inspires the soul by revealing to it its divine creator. So does any noble action, one born in charity and carried out in compassion.

We can do nothing if we hate ourselves, or feel that all our actions are doomed to failure because of our own worthlessness. We have to take ourselves, good and bad alike, on trust before we can do anything. Thus I cannot give of my life to another if I have nothing to give in the first place. The result of a practical self-love is that my attention is no longer fixed on myself with all its defects and inadequacies. Only then can I give my attention wholeheartedly to the other person. But if I am constantly aware of my lack, I will be straining every effort to make that lack good. I will grasp in the most self-centred way to gain the attention and approbation of others. Thus do I boost an inadequate personality by selfish actions. And some of the most selfish acts are those that pass as piety or social philanthropy. This does not mean, of course, that all religious and social action is perverted self-seeking, but it does stress the need for insight into one's own motives and attitude. If I do good in order to assert myself or justify myself in any way or even to attain personal salvation or reach the divine presence on my own, I have no knowledge of love and my actions are mere selfishness. But if I do good without so much as thinking in categories of goodness and evil or of my own standing with man or even with God, then I have begun the painful glorious journey of losing myself for the sake of God. This self has to be lost for its real, eternal counterpart, the soul, to be finally revealed. But it cannot be lost until it is warmly cherished, just as a parent cherishes

its child without in any way being deluded about the child's
goodness.

To acquire this enlightened view of personality is part of the
life of the spirit. Like all the other inner attitudes that transform
our lives and make us worthy servants of God, this changed view
comes from outside. Mere intellectual appreciation is at most
a precursor of understanding. The change of heart, or
"metanoia", comes to us from God. But in order for this to
happen we must be prepared. In other words, the inner life
proceeds by discipline, a discipline by which the soul is dedicated
to God for His service, and not for our benefit. Of course, we do
benefit, but this is not the reason for the quest. When we can
say with St. Paul, "I live; yet not I, but Christ liveth in me,"
then we have truly arrived. For the self that now lives is not
the one which looks for benefits or rewards, but rather one that
has no existence at all except in union with God in Christ, who
is God's eternal word in action throughout the whole created
universe, and Who was with God before the foundation of the
world, and in Whom all created things are to be united and lifted
up into the unity of the Godhead. This disinterested seeking for
God is very important, for a great deal of the "self-development"
that is in current demand is based on occult techniques that tend
to increase personal power without developing the spiritual
nature.

The quiet mind

If one is to approach God in silence, the mind must be still
and at rest. When it is filled with all the world's commerce it
cannot know the one thing that matters. When we speak of knowing, let us use that word in its archaic sense of having an intimate
relationship with someone. We can only "know" in this context
when the mind is quiet and receptive. If only we had that inner
tranquillity we would be filled with that void in which all is
contained. To be still in complete joy and surrender is to be
filled with the Holy Spirit. He is always wanting to enter our
consciousness, but we never seem to be at home in ourselves to
receive Him.

The cultivation of the inner silence is called *meditation*. It is
unnecessary to commend this practice, because it is nowadays
talked about by so many. Yet despite the many teachers of the

subject and the various techniques used, the minds of most people, even experienced meditators, are usually far from the centre where God is known. This is because the attitude and objectives of many of those who meditate are not centred on God but are devoted to the aggrandisement of the isolated self. There is no harm in commencing meditation with a dominating concern for self-improvement, but if through the practice of meditation the perspective of the individual has not transcended the personal to reach the universal, there can be no doubt that the technique is merely one of self-indulgence.

If one wants to meditate, it is important first to place the body at ease, but not in such a posture that sleep can be easily induced. The body must always be glorified. Mortification of the flesh harks back to a mediaeval dualism of flesh and spirit whereby the flesh had to be subjected before the spirit could be in command. A modern spirituality sees that the spirit is best in command of a willing, healthy body which can be progressively resurrected by the enlightened, all-pervading spirit.

Once the body is stilled in comfort and with reverence, the emotions have to be quietened, and the stream of thoughts that traverse and trouble the mind slowly dissipated. To do this is the heart of meditation. It is performed by filling the mind with one thought, or image, or repeated phrase (or even a repeated sound, which is called a mantra). At first the mind may, in its ignorance, try to dissect or analyse the seed of meditation, but it must be instructed to rest on that theme or sound. To stop analysing and criticising and to flow out in active blessing (which is the heart of rest) is the basis of a real relationship.

Meditation is a relationship in the depth of silence with the object of meditation. And when the relationship is complete, subject and object merge into a unity in which the one becomes the other inasmuch as both lose their separate identity and instead are members of the body of creation, which is the universal body of Christ. This is the I-Thou relationship of Martin Buber, in which there is neither subject nor object, but all is one in that ultimate reality which is God.

When this glorious state of union is experienced, the soul is free and in communion with all other souls. It is then that the divine presence may irrupt into the personal consciousness and the soul may know incontrovertibly of the divinity within it. But this is a gift from without; it cannot be grasped by techniques,

no matter how arduous and painstaking they are. The more on
grasps, the more the isolated personality is in command and th
further one is from a knowledge of God. The technique c
meditation is one of progressive self-annihilation so that the spiri
can make itself known in the soul. This is called "contemplation"

In the depth of meditation you begin to know yourself bette
As the outer trappings of personality are shed and the complexe
of the unconscious mind lose their emotional hold on the atten
tion, so the soul lies revealed in its pristine glory. The distractin
elements of the personality can be viewed with a greater perspec
tive which is itself a fruit of the detachment from persona
grasping that comes from meditation. The quiet mind can discer
truth because it is less dominated by the outer world of con
ditioning and the inner world of psychological debris than is th
untrained, distractable mind in everyday life.

He who knows the eloquent silence of meditation is no longe
alone. He is in communion with the unseen world of eternity
with the living and the dead. The communion of saints become
a real experience, and relationships with those still in the fles
assume a greater depth than before.

Thus, the quiet mind is a mind that is fully awake. It is aware
receptive, waiting in reverence for the divine command. "Her
am I. Send me." (Isaiah 6.8). The mind of unawakened man i
asleep even when engaged in furious activity. This is becaus
the unawakened mind is merely a passive cipher of all the un
restrained impulses impinging on it from its unconscious part
It acts not in control but as a mere machine. The quiet mind i
controlled by the soul. It listens more and asserts itself less.

Do not make the mistake of believing that inner tranquillit
and the practice of meditation are means of escaping from th
world's work. If meditation does indeed evoke an attitude o
apathy to the things of the world, the philosophy and practic
underlying it are suspect. The proof of a healthy quietness an
a beneficial type of meditation is an alert, untroubled mind tha
can act positively in every demanding situation. Such a min
listens in attention to another person's troubles, meditating o
these troubles and the person who is afflicted. Proper relation
ships with other people are really meditations upon them an
their problems, not in a separative, analytical frame of mind, bu
in that union of regard which can identify us with the person an

feel direct compassion for him. It is thus that we can be of assistance to another in trouble—not so much by giving infallible advice as by being with him and supporting him during his period of travail.

To be of help to someone, we must first achieve detachment from his problem while having a real commitment to the person himself. We cannot, indeed must not, solve another's problems. Not only are we ignorant of his soul's destiny, but we must also allow that soul to grow into its natural freedom by working out its own salvation; the problem at hand is one milestone on the way. But we can support the person. A real relationship is one of quiet commitment. In this quiet awareness we can do one of the most difficult of all things: we can learn to say "No". True love is stern and unemotional. It is not a doormat to be trampled on by selfish immature people. Not only is this deleterious to oneself, but of even greater importance it hinders the growth into maturity of the other person. Even Jesus had to leave the disciples before the Holy Spirit could enter their consciousness fully, and proceed to lead them into all truth—a function incidentally which is still uncompleted because of the unawakened consciousness of people even today.

As the inner life is cultivated, so we move beyond the isolation of loneliness to an awareness of the unity of all life. Communion with people is now possible because we have no further need for self-assertiveness. And at last we can approach God directly in prayer. This is the culmination of the inner way.

This brings us to the subject of Prayer.

CHAPTER 10

Prayer

PRAYER IS THE SUPREME action of the inner life. It is the communion of the soul with God, the ascent of the mind to God.

Prayer starts as a transient elevation of the mind to the realm of eternity in which the person of God is known, but when prayer life is fully established, you are never far from the divine presence no matter what you are doing. Prayer is, in other words, something much more than a mere setting aside of part of the day for communion with God. It is a way of life in which the human will is consecrated to alignment with the divine will. When this happens, there is a transformation of the personality due to its integration around the focal point of the soul which is called the spirit.

Prayer differs from contemplation in that the person is giving of himself to God in silence. Meditation is a necessary precursor to effective prayer inasmuch as it keeps the mind focussed on the boundless void in which the being of God is known. But prayer is a relationship in which we are giving of our very essence to God—in petition, in intercession, in praise, and above all in silent adoration. Rapt adoration in silent contemplation is the meaning of worship. Religious ritual and liturgy are to be seen as an admirable focus for meditation, so that the soul is now sufficiently stilled to commune with God, who can at last enter into our consciousness.

Unfortunately most liturgies with their copious prayers seem to be an end in themselves, and the worshipper is usually afforded no period of silence in which to perform the act of prayer. In the Hindu-Buddhist tradition, which is far more advanced in its understanding of the inner life of the spirit than is the Western theistic one, a whole scheme of bodily and mental discipline is inculcated as an effective way to reaching that reality in which the ground of existence is known. I refer, of course, to the profound system of yoga that is part of this great religious tradition. But yoga is the way to God—or the ground of being, for those who cannot accept a purely personal God—and not an end in itself. Many Westerners who study Eastern techniques do not see that the end of these systems is *union of the soul with God.* In this union techniques, liturgies, rituals, and even objects of veneration, whether tangible or mental, are left behind. They are gateways to the divine presence, but must not be confused with God. Unfortunately this confused identification is very common in the development of a religious tradition, which almost always degenerates from the inspired vision of the founder to the dogmatic, unimaginative practice of an unenlightened congregation of later times. "The letter killeth, but the spirit giveth life," says St. Paul. It is the Holy Spirit that teaches us how to pray—and indeed prays through us and for us. The techniques of religious traditions are designed to allow the Holy Spirit dominion over the personality, but they are not prayer in themselves.

Prayer starts with the intuitive recognition that there is a power outside human reason that can be approached in simple petition during times of difficulty. It ends in the marriage of the soul with God Who is beyond all categories, and in Whom there is alone complete rest—that rest in which the whole universe is raised up to divine stature. To many people prayer is synonymous with petition. Certainly our first intimation of the divine presence may be the outcome of an intuitional cry into the void of being when we are bereft of worldly help. Even hardened agnostics will invoke the aid of the intangible powers of the universe when they are at breaking point. When our whole personality is fully aware of the difficult situation in which we find ourselves, we are moving beyond the world of fleeting images and vain imaginings to a realm of rapt meditation on a theme—which is our own unhappiness. One cannot pray until the mind is fixed on the object of concern, which in the early stages of one's prayer life is oneself and one's need.

It is important to realise that this type of meditation is part of human life and is not the preserve of the specially trained person. But prayer transcends mere meditation on our own lack or difficulty. It is a presentation of the difficulty to that power which we know in terms of personality as God. This presentation of a deficiency to God, who is an ineffable premise to the intellectually based agnostic, is performed in silence. We cease to be aware even of the ground of our petition and are part of a great silence in which God is known. In the silence a new way of life opens out to us, and we see darkly into a greater future. Thus is prayer answered. If it is undertaken in humble trust, and if it culminates in rapt silence, it sets in motion a sequence of events, mostly on an inner plane in our own personalities, that transforms our lives. But prayer of a stylised extrovert character, in which we, as a matter of habit, invoke God's aid for the projects that are dear to our heart, and even instruct Him how to proceed, achieves nothing, and merely estranges agnostics (and even believers) from the practice of the presence of God, which is the secret of the life of prayer.

There is no aspect of the life of the spirit that demands closer, more critical scrutiny than prayer. It is not the same as saying our prayers, a practice usually inculcated in the young and subsequently abandoned when it appears to be of no real value in our lives. The value of periods of recitation of conventional prayers is that these move the mind away from mundane works to the way of God. But in themselves they hardly take one even to the foothills of the mountain of illumination, and can indeed become a stumbling-block to effective communion with God by dulling the mind with familiar images. Furthermore, much enunciated prayer has strong undertones of superstition. A failure to pray is expected to lead to an unpleasant event.

Of all the adverse effects of religion, superstition is the most dangerous, for it leads to a state of mind in which one believes that God's help can be bargained for by performing stereotyped rituals. Nothing is calculated to diminish the stature of human personality more than a servile submission of our will to the presumed will of God, in the assurance that all will go well for us provided we do as God wishes. Surely it is the divine will that man should grow into that fullness of being which was seen perfectly in the witness of Christ, in His life, ministry, passion, and resurrection. Thus there can be only one real prayer of petition, that we may be led through the power of the Holy Spirit into ever deeper communion with God. In other words, there is only one fully realised prayer: union of God and man so that there is a union in man of the human and divine natures as was made manifest in the incarnate Christ. All petitions end in union with God. Then the petitions are swallowed up in the reality of eternal life.

The effect of prayer is that our perspective in life is no longer held at personal, subjective aims. It is raised to God, in Whom alone perfection is to be seen. This does not mean that we go beyond worldly things, freeing ourselves from the claims of the flesh and of earthly matter, but that we see the divine nature in every manifestation of life, and that our work, no matter how dull it appears to be by superficial appearances, becomes infused with God. This is the splendid vision of the mystic, that God is in all His creation, and we, in union with Him, can participate in the transfiguration of matter. The key to constructive living is not to escape from the limitations of the world into a private realm of bliss but to raise up all the creation to that bliss which is eternal life. This is love in action, the union of the human with the divine will. It is the abundant life. "The universe itself is to be freed from the shackles of mortality and enter upon the liberty and splendour of the children of God," writes St. Paul. In this vision of the consummation of all things in Christ, personal petition pales into insignificance, except inasmuch as we pray to become better, more profitable servants. Thus the petition that is worth something is that we may be infused with faith, compassion, and that love which alone can bring the experience of forgiveness. If we desire the experience of union with God we should pray to be more loving in our human relationships. The second great commandment reinforces the first, while the first makes the second possible.

In silent prayer the intimate communion that exists between all creation and God becomes tangible to the soul. That we are all members one of another is certain in the experience of the true self. For my identity, though unique, achieves reality only in relationship to the whole body of mankind. Thus the soul is, unlike the outer personality that encloses it in form, never circumscribed or alone. It is in psychic communion with all other souls and in spiritual communion with God.

This understanding is important in relation to intercessory prayer. When we remember another in prayer we are not asking a vengeful personal God to help or forgive a sinner whom He is punishing. We are establishing communion with the other person on the level of the soul, and the agent that communicates is the Holy Spirit. Prayer is indeed the deepest (and most exalted) type of relationship. Instead of achieving a mere sensory contact, as occurs in everyday life when we meet another person, or even an extrasensory one, as occurs sporadically through telepathy with someone whom we know very well, there is a spiritual communication at the deepest level of the soul. Intercessory prayer is a much more exalted relationship than a mere telepathic rapport, for it goes beyond circumscribed personality to embrace all people. Thus I can pray for a complete stranger, but I cannot have telepathic communication except with someone I already know. Telepathy works on the level of the soul-infused personality, whereas intercessory prayer is of the spark of the soul, which mystics call the spirit. This distinction underlines the separation of psychic and spiritual levels of awareness. Both are of the soul, but whereas the first is purely personal, the second transcends personality to embrace all men (and eventually all the universe) in selfless love. Whenever we remember another person in loving concern, we are praying for him.

The communion of man and God so rejoices the soul that it flows out in praise to God, Who has been the author of the transforming relationship. This praise is usually silent, and it emanates as a radiance from the spiritual aspirant. It may also be enunciated aloud, even with the unintelligible speaking in tongues. This is a language of praise in which the reasoning mind is overruled by a more basic intuitive awareness of Deity. It responds by praise that far exceeds the range of the intellect. Such "charismatic prayer" can be a liberating experience so long as it is seen to be merely a stage in the spiritual life. But it becomes incarcerating when it is accepted as the height of prayer.

Deep silence is the medium of real communication. Words, even sincere praise, can exalt the personality of the aspirant while obliterating that silence in which alone the voice of God reveals itself. The Holy Spirit is our mentor in prayer. He leads us from the restriction of the reasoning mind to the free flow of emotional response and finally to the awesome silence where God may reveal Himself to us as overwhelming love and uncreated light. Prayer is of love and shares love's properties; it is selfless, aware only of the other, and leads all into freedom.

Prayer is as necessary for the soul as air is for the body. The fruit of prayer is vision; the action of prayer is love.

Prayer and guidance

As we have already noted with regard to spiritual growth in everyday life, a test of the greatest severity meets us whenever we have to make a decision of moment. Such a decision may not only change the course of our own lives but may also have irrevocable effects on those around us, especially the people who depend on us and whom we love dearly. In coming to the decision which we hope will be "right", it is a natural reaction to pray to God for guidance. Once again, when our rational faculties can no longer solve the problem—and this occurs soon in any dilemma of significance—we intuitively seek the obscurity within us wherein lies dormant, yet potentially revealed, the spark of God. It is worth considering the response of the soul to the request for divine guidance, for in this important exercise lie revealed many sources of false inspiration as well as authentic guidance from the Holy Spirit.

A fairly common result of inner petition for help is the manifestation of a voice that instructs. This voice may be an inner teacher who communicates intelligible information, or it may have the sensory quality of an external guide. The question is whether the guidance is of God or from some other source. This is where testing the spirits is a vital part of the spiritual life. All information coming to us in the silence of meditation arises from the unconscious part of the mind. It may indeed also originate there from one of the many conflicts and complexes of the past that lie buried in the deeper recesses of the mind. Or it may come from some external source close to one. This may be another person with whom one is in close psychic rapport, or it may be of discarnate origin, from the mind of a deceased person or even from some other entity in the realm of the unseen world.

Most spiritualistic communication arises from this typically psychic level of reality. The value of the teaching given is neither as low as antagonists of psychism assert nor as exalted as most confirmed spiritualists believe. But to rely on this source of guidance when a decision of moment has to be made is unwise at the very least. People who go to outer oracles for guidance, or even find an inner oracle of this type in themselves, become insidiously enslaved to powerful psychic influence to the cost of their own development into full, mature human beings. It might be noted here that some of these sources of information are regarded as divine by those who rely on them. These deluded people believe quite sincerely that they are in touch with God, who speaks directly to them and tells them what to do.

But there is also another source of guidance from the unconscious mind, and this is the Holy Spirit, Who comes to our consciousness from the spark of the soul (or the spirit where God is immanent, and where the fact of God is known). In the height of contemplative (or mystical) prayer we are fully tractable to the Holy Spirit, for our concern is no longer bounded by personal considerations. "I live; yet not I, but Christ liveth in me." This state is know as "rapt prayer" though, of course, it is not held for any length of time except by those who are advanced on the spiritual path. The Holy Spirit can then lead us to the truth of the situation. He does not tell us what to do in a dictatorial way. Nor does He provide infallible instructions. He suffuses our soul with the warmth of love and the light of wisdom, so that we, as fully integrated people, can now make the appropriate decision ourselves, using intellect, emotion, and the intuition that comes from the soul as one coherent unit. Thus we understand the great statement of St. Paul, "Where the Spirit of the Lord is, there is liberty." He leads us into truth by leading us into the fullness of personality, whose guiding light is the spirit of the soul. When a decision is made on this level of awareness, we are so full of divine grace that we have the faith to leave the results in God's hands and merely do the best we can at that particular moment of time. This is the type of guidance that prayer evokes.

This consideration is also important in assessing the origin and quality of the "gifts of the Spirit" that St. Paul speaks about in 1 Corinthians 12, and that are so much sought after in the modern charismatic movement. There is no doubt that when the reasoning mind is deposed from its seat of authority—and how it clings there in Western society—the personality can become responsive to other influences. Some of these are frankly demonic in character, as is seen typically in mentally deranged people. But those who abdicate the reason by sacrifice in faith are now treading a new path—by a hidden light they are moving towards fullness of being. This is the way of spiritual progress. If you want to be tractable to the Holy Spirit, you must give of yourself unreservedly, but under no condition must you repudiate your personal attributes, which include the intellect. These attributes, and especially the intellect, must be fully active but under the guidance of the soul. Then the inspiration which flows into the personality can be used properly and purposefully. Not all the inspiration comes directly from the Holy Spirit; some of it comes from the psychic world, as I have already explained. This is by no means to be deprecated, for much of it is of high quality. Indeed, the gifts of the Spirit are basically psychical. But if the Holy Spirit is the final source of the soul's inspiration, we shall be led to greater degrees of understanding and wisdom. Above all, we shall radiate the three great virtues: faith, hope, and love. Just as St. Paul's great poem on love (1 Corinthians 13) forms the zenith of his discourse on the gifts of the Spirit, so a truly charismatic individual emanates a love that transcends personal, doctrinal, and racial differences, and brings all men together. This is a measure of the power of the Holy Spirit in the life of man.

I said earlier that petition made in faith is always heard and answered. Let the petition therefore be carefully considered before it is prayed over. A petition that we may be better servants of man and God, and therefore filled with those great qualities we lack, notably faith and love, is one that leads us to God. All petitions centred on personal salvation without reference to the greater body of mankind are divisive. The faith of him who prays brings the petition to God, Who acts to strengthen the soul and bind together the broken personality. This inner integration of the pieces of personality into an entire whole under the guidance of the spirit within constitutes the kingdom of God within each man.

When the kingdom of God and its righteousness is sought in this way, all manner of petitions will be granted. But by the very nature of the healed personality, these petitions will no longer be self-centred and vain. They will be centred on our love of humanity and our worship of God.

Having looked deeply into the meaning of real prayer and real guidance, we must now consider the meaning of real faith.

CHAPTER II

The agnosticism of real faith

OUR WORLDLY LIFE IS a journey in darkness to a visionary destination glimpsed in the heights of aspiration but not illuminated by rational light. It is therefore not to be wondered at that most intellectuals adopt a distinctively sceptical attitude towards the question of meaning in life. They deride all intuitions of a greater glory to be revealed in mankind as childish wishful thinking undertaken to escape the unpalatable fact of the disintegration of the whole personality that awaits us all when the body dies. Religion is seen to be a means of escape from the harsh reality of man's mortality into an ethereal world of personal comfort. The only faith that an atheistic humanist has is that of the potential raising of human endeavour and performance to ever higher standards of excellence. But since, in this type of approach, human consciousness is limited to the physical body, the fate of the individual is one of complete obliteration once earthly life is over. The atheistic view of human destiny is even more depressing than that of the most exclusive religious sects, who at least look for the preservation of a selected group of believers in an after-life state. "Where there is no vision the people perish." The vision of those who cannot see God cannot help man to attain his own full development as a person.

The religionist, by contrast, has a lively faith. This may be grounded in the teaching of a particular scripture, or the tradition of a church, or even the message that emanates from an inspired source. In the theistic tradition God is seen as revealing Himself to mankind on certain momentous occasions. This revelation has to be accepted absolutely if our life in God is to proceed. The plethora of authoritarian groups that have arisen since man first became aware of the transcendent reality that is called God, is a living testimony to the will to believe that is such an important part of human personality. The mutual exclusiveness of many such groups must make the seeker after truth doubt the authenticity of any of their teachings. But the simple folk who require a dogma to live by, even if they do not understand its real meaning, often become enthusiastically responsive to sectarian "faith". Many receive strength by a narrow faith, but few rise through it to a fullness of personality. It is evident that we proceed into the unknown by faith, but that blind faith in a metaphysical position can truncate the full personality.

Faith is not a short cut to salvation. It is to be seen as the guide of the personality on its path to healing. Faith is a gift of God. Like love it can never be evoked from the personality. It can only be invoked by prayer. Faith is implanted in the spirit of man. It is a tiny light that leads us through the darkness that encompasses and defeats the reasoning mind. "I would not seek thee had I not found thee," says Pascal with profound insight. Faith is the movement of the personality towards that integration which is accomplished by the spirit of the soul. To choose the nobler of two ways of life, to exalt the good above the mean or the beautiful above the meretricious is an act of faith. The soul lies revealed when we move by faith, for we are leaving behind the categories of intellectual knowledge based on past experience, and are treading an unknown path.

The spiritual quest is a continuous act of faith, a faith that spiritual experience is the most real thing in human life and that all other categories of experience are subordinate to the fact of God. To move in fear and trembling through the dark tragedies that punctuate human life with the inner knowledge that all will be well at an indeterminable future period, is the pinnacle of faith. This acceptance of the fundamental goodness of the universe despite all rational indications to the contrary is the faith that saves. It bears a close relationship to the love that comes to us from God when we are empty enough of conceit to receive it.

The most important quality of real faith is its tendency to integrate the personality and make the person more mature in all his attitudes. It does not demand a surrender or denial of the body, the reasoning mind, or the emotions. A faith that diminishes one's power of private judgment and forces one, beyond all reason, to accept a dogmatic teaching on trust, is not likely to integrate the personality. On the contrary, by denying a most important part of the personality, the reason, it diminishes the person and makes him a puppet forced to accept various propositions for his own "salvation". This is the criticism of authoritarian religion: it imprisons the person so that his intellectual growth is stultified. If through imposed faith a person cannot face the various facts of life honestly and without prejudice, that faith prevents the full maturing of his personality. Far from bringing Christ to the individual, it replaces Him with some finite theological proposition or material image. It prevents that total giving of oneself in real selfless faith, a giving that is the precursor of the divine revelation within the soul.

It follows then that the spiritual life proceeds by faith in the gifts bestowed on us by God. These gifts are first of all the glory of the world round us and the people whom we love. But apart from such tangible evidence of God's grace, there are also the intimations of divine reality that come to us from the unseen world. These lighten the burdened heart and revive the flagging spirit within us. These give us assurance of God's concern even when we are feeling at our worst. The supreme gift of mystical insight is an extension of this assurance of personal validity and meaning into a realm of eternity. Thus does the intimation of the glory to be revealed in us first impinge on our awareness, and start a quiet transformation of the personality. The positive polarity of faith is accepting these intimations with gratitude and working through them towards that change of heart which is the measure of spiritual integrity. But, as we already noted in connexion with prayer, these sudden flights from the stultifying world of everyday life into a new way of release must be studied carefully with the critical faculty of the reasoning mind. A ray of light in a dark atmosphere must always be acknowledged, but its guiding tendency must be carefully assessed. This is the negative polarity of real faith. It is a passionate agnosticism which endeavours with all ardour to gauge the truth and meaning of the revelation.

The distinction between a life-enhancing experience of God and a self-enhancing psychical experience can be extremely difficult, and in some instances acknowledged mental instability adds a further complication to the assessment.

Faith and suggestion

It is a well-known psychological principle that ideas implanted into our mind can produce corresponding physical effects. Thus a true therapeutic relationship between doctor and patient or between analyst and analysand can produce beneficial effects apart from any positive treatment that may be given. The old-fashioned bedside manner, now greatly derided by a scientifically orientated generation, undoubtedly helped many ill patients towards recovery. Of course, this close relationship in a healing undertaking is no substitute for scientific accuracy, and is rightly suspected by all intelligent observers. Indeed, it is well recognised that inert material masquerading as a powerful drug can have a remarkably ameliorative effect in many chronic diseases, but in due course the benefit wears off and the patient relapses once more. The powerful effect of one personality on another is the basis of suggestion, and it can sometimes become attached to a drug, a technique, or a religious ritual. While no one would deny the power of this primitive type of "faith" in the healing of various disabilities, there can be no doubt that it does tend to diminish the personality of the seeker inasmuch as it interferes with his own powers of discernment. In a true healing relationship—and this is the basis of paranormal, or psychic healing—there is not simply a blind subservience to the personality of the healer but rather an outflow of psychic energy from the healer to the afflicted person. This energy comes from the soul and enters the soul whence it is directed to the entire personality. We know far too little about man's psychic constitution to make definite statements about healing on a psychic level, but it seems that a relationship is the key to the healing act. Suggestion acts rather on the mental than the psychical level, but it too plays an important part in all forms of healing.

The recitation of phrases that emanate "positive thinking" is recommended by some practitioners of the various types of "new thought". While the sentiments contained in many such repeated phrases and sentences are admirable, they sometimes tend to lull the person's own self-awareness and exalt him far above his true station in the spiritual life. The automatic repetition of self-inflating material does no final good, but a meditation on some great theme or sentence from the Bible (or other scripture) may help to calm the mind and make us more integrated than we were before. Thus the uncritical recitation of material, however noble it may appear, takes the centre of being away from the person himself, and focuses it on an external source of authority. Nevertheless, this type of exercise can be of the greatest value to those in severe mental distress who are so imprisoned in a web of self-denigration and gloom that they are quite unable to see the light of God's glory in the world around them. To such people the recitation of a great sentence from the Bible can be an anchor-hold of sanity in the shifting sands of material life. Thus, we should never adopt a destructive attitude towards means of self-development that may help others through particularly difficult periods of life. But we must also, in due charity, see the limitation of this approach to truth, and in due course move beyond it. Suggestion is in fact a first-aid treatment for those near breaking-point. At least they can grasp on to a tangible object of security. But they should not identify this object with God. And in due course they should move beyond reliance on an external aid to the source of inspiration within themselves.

Religious faith and spirituality

If religion were doing what it purports to do, it would lead man to an encounter with God. In fact, in the world around us there are many spiritually aspiring people who have, through bitter experience, dispensed with the services of all organised churches and have joined in the larger communion of man dedicated to God's service. This is a sad state of affairs, for membership of a church ought to lead one to worship God in the fellowship of other believers. Instead, the whole approach of much conventional religion tends to obscure the fact of God with man-made rituals and theological niceties. While the experts retreat into their own doctrinal preserves, the mass of humanity is left to find God on its own.

It is noteworthy that the three friends whom I mentioned in an earlier chapter had no connexion with any church. Though they were all brought up in the Christian tradition, the breadth of their sympathies and the range of their minds made the limitations of any one religious system unbearable. I feel that this was sad from their point of view inasmuch as the love of a congregation of like-minded people could have supported them in their lonely journey and also acted as a centre of constructive criticism in regard to their work and general attitude to life. For no one is so self-sufficient as to be beyond the help of other people. But their absence from the organised church was even sadder from the point of view of traditional religion. These souls, true prophets of the coming age, could have been of immeasurable value in broadening the minds of the all too smug conventional churchgoer and heightening the vision of the church.

A church of whatever religious tradition should be the place where the tension between traditional values and prophetic insight is experienced and resolved, and a new synthesis established. In fact it is usually a place of the "establishment", bent above all else in maintaining the status quo (which is usually wrongly equated with orthodoxy) and fearful of any manifestation of the Holy Spirit, whose work it is to lead us all progressively into greater understanding of the truth. Jesus Himself is recorded as saying that there were many things He could not tell the disciples, for they could not, in their present state of understanding, bear to hear them. It was the function of the Holy Spirit to continue this work of leading people into the truth.

Through the centuries the Holy Spirit has performed this life-giving work, and He has chosen all manner of people to be His agents. Not only has He worked through the saints and theologians, but He has also been the inspiration of the artists, scientists, psychologists, and philosophers who have led men into a greater understanding and control of their environment and especially of themselves. Quite a number of those whom the Holy Spirit has inspired have not been religionists at all, and a few have been militant atheists! Indeed, some of the images of God that have been constructed by the theistic religions are so harmful to human progress that it has been necessary for God to destroy them. God's professed enemies are of small account, but His devoted friends have so little faith in His own omnipotence that they seek all too often to bolster Him up with vain theologies, often repulsive to human nature. The terrible wars and persecutions undertaken in the name of religion—and they are with us even today—testify to the demonic aspect of man's search for God. It is noteworthy also that the Western theistic tradition has an infinitely more horrible record of cruelty in this respect than has the Hindu-Buddhist tradition, which being mystically aware, can see beyond personality to ultimate reality.

The religious quest is for truth. In the name of truth people will not only sacrifice their lives but also calmly destroy others whom they call heretics. This tendency to heresy hunting has departed to a great extent from the realm of organised religion (which is at present a comparatively weak force in the world at large, though there are important exceptions), and is more the preserve of political and economic ideologies that have evoked so much emotional fervour that they could be regarded as new religions. Marxism and its variants come clearly into this category. To be in possession of the whole truth is man's final ideal. Since in God the qualities of truth, goodness (or love), and beauty merge and find their ultimate manifestation, it is commendable, at its very least, to seek after truth. The scientist searches on a material level, the psychologist on a mental one, and the religionist looks for the consummation of all truth in God.

There is one certain quality of truth. It illuminates the reason by broadening its range. It shines on the intellect, increasing the scope of the mind and raising the personality to the awareness of the soul within it. Indeed, truth, far from being a finite point of destination, is the open-ended way that leads to God. It is the way of perfection, and as a new aspect of truth is revealed to us, so the past view that we believed was the final truth has to be reviewed and modified according to the new information. "I am the way, the truth, and the life" (John 14.6). The path, the destination, and the will are all one in God.

Clement of Alexandria saw a threefold movement of the human soul towards the truth that is God. We start in faith, progress to knowledge, and ultimately proceed by love. Love is the most exalted knowledge, for it is unitive. It transcends the separation of men and establishes a communion between them with God as the centre point as well as the totality of the relationship. Thus faith in any finite presentation of the truth is divisive and illusory, for other people will be guided to see other aspects of the same truth. And each view of the truth, being exclusive in its claims of absolute authority, will war with the other. It follows that a faith dependent on an intellectual or theological position is never complete, and as we grow in spiritual stature so the faith broadens. The spiritual life makes the aspirant increasingly tractable to the Holy Spirit, who leads us into the truth of God through the cosmic Christ.

It can therefore be said that the most real religion is that which brings fullness of being to the person. Instead of making him rely on externally imposed doctrines and formulations, it inspires his soul to a clearer vision of the ultimate truth of God. Whatever is said or taught about Him is a mere commentary on His being, which is experienced in love, not ratiocination. "By love may he be gotten and holden, but by thought never," says the writer of *The Cloud of Unknowing*. We love as we become more receptive to God's love, which flows most fully into the integrated, cleansed personality. A personality full of intellectual blockages based on dogmatic views of God's nature and purpose excludes the divine marriage within. Nothing is easier than to exclude God from our being by identifying Him with dogmatic statements or credal formulae.

The value of a religious tradition is that it balances the insights bestowed upon the believer by the Holy Spirit with the past experience of the human race down the ages. Not every insight is divinely inspired. As already noted, some revelations are of unconscious material flooding into consciousness, and others are of indeterminate psychic origin that varies considerably in its degree of inspiration. A well-trodden path of spirituality has been preserved for us by the saints and prophets of all the major religious traditions. Only a very rash person will ignore the witnesses of the cosmic Christ down the ages. But no past teaching or experience is to be regarded as final. Substance becomes shadow as a greater substance lies revealed. And the greatest substance is that which is beyond limitation, whose being is the void in which all creation occurs and proceeds to eternity. This is the God to whom the whole created universe moves in eager expectation.

As, in faith, you allow the Holy Spirit to lead your progressively integrated personality into a greater understanding of truth, so the eternal meaning of the world's inspired scriptures will become more plain. There is one truth and that is the fact of God. Scriptural inspiration (or revelation, as some would prefer to call it) is a testimony to the divine indwelling in the souls of those great men of a past age. Their witness speaks not only of the eternal Godhead but also of the human condition, which though it varies according to the period of time and the cultural tradition in which it finds itself, is also essentially the same throughout all ages. Since human life began man has always been confronted with the fact of his own mortality and the living changelessness of the Most High. Man's response to this, his faith, and his hope of immortality, vary in form from age to age, but the substance remains unaltered. The validity of the highest religious teaching impresses itself directly upon the liberated soul. "Beloved now are we the sons of God, and it doth not yet appear what we shall be : but we know that when he shall appear we shall be like him, for we shall see him as he is" (I John 3.2). It is thus that a free faith leads to a proper discernment of spirits.

In assessing religious truth the two pitfalls to be avoided are a dogmatic fundamentalism which accepts a literal view on "faith" despite the protesting groans of the reasoning part of the mind, and an obsessive modernism which tries above all else to be "with it". Such an attitude to religious truth becomes subservient to current scientific and philosophical trends to the extent that it is ashamed of its own witness and dubious of its validity. Spiritual truth never denies or contradicts reason. It extends rational thought by new intuitive insights. Thus the healing power of Jesus and other great figures in religious history is neither to be seen as a special miraculous revelation of God nor as an aspect of pre-scientific superstition. It was rather a testimony to the power inspired by the Holy Spirit into a fully integrated personality under the direction of the spirit within.

The creeds and sacraments of the church need therefore not be dismissed as relics of pre-scientific thinking or old-fashioned superstition. They express eternal truth, but they are not static formulations. They are the repository of mystery—the ineffable encounter between God and man—and when approached in awe they may yield to the humble soul priceless spiritual riches. But all higher religion is to be seen as God's gift to man. Jesus said that He did not come to destroy the law but to fulfil it. He also declared that that most sacred of Jewish institutions, the Sabbath, was made for man, and not man for the Sabbath. If we follow the way of tradition with a receptive soul and an actively responsive reason, we will be enabled, through the Holy Spirit, to distil what is really vital from the past while discerning that which is questionable. This latter is, to a large measure, the accretion of a later period when the religious genius had decayed, and faith was replaced by superstitious fear and arrogant exclusiveness.

The spiritual man's faith will lead him into all truth, as he moves with fear and trembling—and yet at the same time fearlessly—into the unknown day's work ahead of him. The humble heart, the adventurous spirit, the questioning mind, the vibrant body—these are our instruments of fulfilment. The faith to proceed is given to us as we work in dedication to the great quest. Externally enforced systems are at the least redundant, and often frankly harmful to the spirit of man. "Quench not the Spirit," but have the wisdom to discern its origin.

CHAPTER 12

The social roots of the spirit

IT COULD BE OBSERVED, and with some justification too, that the quest for spiritual enlightenment seems to take one away from the world and its cogent concerns into a rarefied existence in which the purity of ultimate reality is enjoyed without the jarring presence of mundane life. Of course, this accusation has been levelled in the past, and not always without some truth, against enclosed religious orders and even against the religious life in general. I am, in this account of the quest for God, writing quite definitely as a layman to laymen, for I believe that the constant interplay between spiritual aspiration and active participation in the world's commerce is the authentic way towards a knowledge of God. Those whose vocation is towards the contemplative life in an enclosed community are in no way belittled by this assertion. Their path is a special one, and its validity is to be judged by the product that emerges from it and the power of prayer it produces for the world's good.

No one living in the contemporary scene can be oblivious of the mounting problems of humanity. In one respect these have always been with us on account of the ambivalence of human nature, but, of course, the immense technological developments that have ensued from the recent scientific revolution have not only changed the face of the earth but have also challenged many comfortable assumptions about the independence and uniqueness of the human being. It is worth meditating on some of the problems that confront us all as members of the human race.

There is first of all the ominous growth of population throughout the world, itself largely the outcome of the eradication of much infectious disease, such as tuberculosis, malaria, and yellow fever, which killed large numbers of young in previous eras. The gradual victory over malnutrition in developed countries has added to the population problem. To offset this, many people are taking advantage of methods of birth control, and indiscriminate abortion is now practised in many parts of the world. While these methods certainly reduce the density of the population, they also leave in their wake a degrading view of human life. Is man merely a hypersexed animal whose chief function it is to enjoy himself without responsibility to the higher demands of life?

The overcrowding germane to the population explosion is augmented by the means of rapid inter-continental travel, some of it comparatively cheap and now available to nearly everyone. Not only is the world a much smaller place than it appeared to our forefathers, but it is becoming increasingly difficult to escape from the uproar all round us into a haven of quiet and peace. A rapidly developing population is seldom properly educated in the niceties of living. Whereas in previous ages a small aristocracy lived in luxury while an enormous working class subsisted at near starvation level, there has recently been a progressive levelling out of privilege and opportunity among the various classes of the population, at least in Western society.

This transmutation of personal privilege to common legal right, while thoroughly commendable in terms of social justice, has brought in its trail a whole generation of well-educated young people who have no immediate work of real value or inspiration to look forward to. Thus there is a general feeling of aimlessness, fruitlessness, and disillusionment amongst a generation who are immensely privileged when compared with their forebears. To escape from the nonentity of faceless safety in a welfare state, many turn to drugs, many to ecstatic religious cults which produce a pseudo-mystical experience that dulls the reasoning mind, and some even to crime.

A growing population loses contact with the soil from which it originally came. The earth is ravaged, the atmosphere is polluted, animals are destroyed and exploited for human greed, and a waste-land emerges to harmonise with the waste-land of the disregarded human soul. To face this vision of darkness some take to nihilistic despair, while others look for an authoritarian political system in which the God-given freedom of the person is subordinated to the claims of the monolithic state.

Here are at least a few of the intellectually insoluble problems of our own time. What use is the witness of the individual, be he ever so saintly and spiritually aware, amid this human wilderness? Will automation, which in many ways seems to eclipse human mentality, give people enough leisure to destroy themselves by vice, or will they emerge with a heightened awareness of the reality that underlies all outer appearances? It all depends on the witness and faith of the aspirant.

The first thing to realise is that these immense problems are outside the solution of any one person or group. Their origin lies in the unredeemed nature of most men who seek personal gain rather than the common good. It is very easy to adopt a sanctimonious view of the sins of society when one is comfortable and at ease, but one's attitude is very different when one's own possessions and way of life are challenged. Then one springs to the defensive intent on establishing the status quo. But the spiritually alive person is aware of something else, namely that there is a power behind the cosmic flow which is all-powerful and all-caring. This is God, and in Him alone can there be redemption.

Now God will never take the initiative on earth without human co-operation. Thus the type of religious thinking that relies on God to act and save the world as a distant potentate behind the scenes is foolish. God acts through His agents, who are spiritually aware human beings. It is this awareness of the divine purpose underlying all cosmic action, no matter how terrible some of it appears, that characterises the consciousness of an aspiring man. And the awareness manifests itself in the person's soul as the warmth of hope and the light of faith. If everything in the world, or for that matter in the tiny domain that we call our own life, depended on us alone, we would collapse mentally and physically almost at once through the terrible strain imposed on us by circumstances. But if we are in the loving power of God, we share the burden with Him. He does not take it away from us in some miraculous fashion, but He fills us with the power of the Holy Spirit so that we can act calmly, wisely, and effectively to solve the difficulty or bear the burden. "Yea, though I walk through the valley of the shadow of death, I will fear no evil; for thou art with me."

It follows that the aspirant, though fully aware of the world's burdens and devoid of sentimental under-estimations of the difficulties involved, is nevertheless infused with the joy that radiates directly from the soul. He can act in an emergency, when the whole world appears to be collapsing around him, with quiet confidence. He can see the glory of eternity interpenetrating the misery around him, and thereby inspire those whom he is assisting with a precious vision of the meaning of life—a vision based not on words or formalised belief but on his own personality. When you are really inspired by God, you lose your concern for self and also the feeling of revolt against the fact of suffering that jars so much in the mind of an intellectually based person, and you identify yourself with the work on hand, no matter how vast it is.

The dimension of social problems

How does the life of the spirit help in the battle against social injustice and racial discrimination? First of all, it is necessary that those moving towards divine reality should not only be aware of current social problems but also be knowledgeable about their roots and their true dimensions. Advocates both of the status quo and of a revolutionary change in society are notoriously one-sided. The traditionalist, who is identified with a rigid convention in religion that is all too often miscalled orthodoxy, is incapable of discerning the movement of the Holy Spirit, and strives for the virtues of stability and piety of a past age. The revolutionary, identified nowadays with extreme religious radicalism, is so propelled by emotional fervour that, in his enthusiasm for reform, he loses contact with the facts of human nature. The traditionalist has a basically gloomy view of humanity, and looks for government by a superior class or group in society, whereas the radical often falls into the plausible error of egalitarianism, which believes that all men are alike in their qualities and equal in potentiality.

The bitter experience of life refutes this kindly, but essentially immature, view of human nature. While we believe that all men are equal in God's love, it is nevertheless certain that only a few are in any way capable of reciprocating that love in selfless service to their fellows. Tradition is a well-trodden path of experience through the ages. It is ignored at our peril, but the path does not end at any one epoch. It proceeds onwards, and is indeed fashioned further by those of all successive generations. Its destination is the meeting of man and God. Thus it has no temporal or earthly ending.

When a spiritually aspiring person is confronted with obvious social injustice, such as racial or religious discrimination, there should be no doubt where his sympathies lie, nor should he fail to be counted among the righteous. But his attitude, and therefore the direction of his activity, should be of a more enlightened type than that of the emotional rabble-rouser. Those whose sympathies are with the downtrodden are often fighting an inner battle with the society that nurtured them. If you have had an unfortunate upbringing it is all too easy to identify the pillars of society with your own parents or teachers, and in turn to identify yourself with the underprivileged and weak. Thus what appears on the surface to be a spiritual fight for justice and decency can in fact be a personal vendetta against the establishment. The hallmarks of this type of social action are its fanaticism, its lack of real concern for people as such, and its devotion to doctrinaire panaceas.

It must be said, with regret, that much of the social agitation that is prominent nowadays has this humourless, loveless, grim fanaticism about it. What its protagonists really care about is their political ideology. The people on whose behalf they are agitating are mere ciphers. They are described as "the masses", and this is indeed what they are to this type of individual—masses of human animals to be directed without real consultation into such situations as are judged best for them by these very arrogant, yet emotionally immature theorists.

The seeker after God never loses contact with the person in his concern for society. Thus while it is very easy, and thoroughly satisfying too, to wax hot over social injustices in distant parts of the world, it is a much greater test of our integrity to behave charitably in a local situation. We can all throw up our hands in horror at the monstrous discrimination based on a fellow human being's colour or religion that occurs in foreign parts. But how many of us are loving to the stranger within our own gates? It is unfortunately true that most antagonists of social injustice are impelled more by hatred of the existing order and those that maintain it than by a compassion towards those who suffer under it.

This attitude is of great importance in terms of the ultimate solution of the problem. The man who hates what he calls evil will foment a revolution that destroys everything, good and bad alike, and brings in its turn a new tyranny. And yet the tyranny is as old as history itself, for it is simply the old Adam in man masquerading under a new name—and our current world is full of ideologies, some of the political right and others of the left, that tyrannise gullible men looking pathetically for political salvation, when the only real salvation is of God.

This does not mean that bad governments and corrupt societies are to be tolerated. Of course they must go, and be replaced by those of greater probity and compassion. The sacred history of the Jews, as is clear in the candid pages of the Old Testament, is one of the power of the Holy Spirit speaking through the prophets and denouncing dishonesty and hypocrisy. Old dynasties are swept away as a new ideal of justice emerges. And the final advent is the incarnate Christ Himself. The movement of the spirit is therefore not a mere sweeping aside of one form of injustice so that it can be replaced by another equally odious injustice flourishing under a new, more pretentious name. It is one in which the vision of the people is raised from the limitation of the small, the petty, and the mean to a broader view of man's destiny in Christ. When a spiritual man espouses the cause of the world's wronged and rejected, he does not lose sight of their oppressors. A compassion passes from him that unites oppressor and oppressed, guilty and innocent, into a new creation. He judges less and loves more.

The call in the world's present period of civil and international strife is not so much for the knife of justice as for the embracing arm of reconciliation. It is clear that no particular ethnic group bears all the blame for persecution, nor is any the completely innocent victim of suffering. Likewise, no religious group has been entirely guiltless of provocation through arrogant exclusiveness. We all have much to repent for in our past and present attitudes. The spiritual man realises this in his combat against injustice. He has passed beyond the naïve and destructive self-righteousness that informs less aware people. "For all have sinned, and come short of the glory of God"—this statement of St. Paul is the basis of the spiritual approach to social action. It tries to unite all people, rich and poor, black and white, Jew and gentile, into a larger body of mankind, the material (as well as the mystical) body of Christ in which all are one, while at the same time working out their own salvation with fear and trembling.

The way of life

The quest of God does not demand a retreat from the world or its problems. Far from it; there must be an ever more passionate commitment of the person to the service of his brothers —who, as St. Francis of Assisi saw, include not only human beings but also the whole sentient universe. We cannot ignore the animal creation, nor can we create havoc with our environment by the selfish destruction of vegetation to suit our immediate needs. The threat of pollution is another warning to man of the limited world he inhabits. Even space travel does not seem, at least in terms of the foreseeable future, to offer man much further territory to colonise. We are forced back more and more on the limited range of our planet, and if we pollute it sufficiently, we shall all die. But life will go on even if the human species kills itself, though this would be a tragedy in terms of the process of evolution.

In fact, the spiritually aware person is not a harbinger of gloom, for he sees the power of God in all things. Behind the despair of so much worldly life lies the radiant glow of hope that comes to us from the divine outpouring. Fortunately man is not alone. Even when he does the most outrageous things, there is the power of God, that works as the Holy Spirit in him and in others, that redeems an apparently lost situation, and brings man back to reason once more. The spark of God works in the souls of men, who, usually against their better judgment, do the right thing in the end. The right decision and the appropriate response come not from us but through us as the outpouring of God's grace in us.

The things of this world are to be enjoyed while we, being in the flesh, are partakers of the world. The key to successful living is balance. Moderation, the golden mean, the middle way of the Buddhist, is the way to liberation. Gluttony enslaves the body to its coarser appetites, while asceticism leads to a separation of the soul from the body, which is a sacred organism also. We cannot, during our transient sojourn on the earth, live without preying on the life around us, nor should we be sad about this. All growing things progress by sacrificing themselves for the good of others. Jesus Himself gave mankind His body and His blood in a very real sense that it might be healed through a knowledge of the love of God.

But this use of the world's resources for our own existence must be made with reverence. As little suffering as possible ought to be inflicted, remembering that in the acute sensitivity of the human conscience the suffering of the world is mirrored. The world is a very beautiful place and also a terrifying one. Nothing is more terrifying than a brutalised human being. Nothing is more beautiful than a noble one. "The glory of God is a living man," wrote St. Irenaeus. And his life revives the life of all the world around him.

As we grow in the spiritual life so we come to realise that our greatest service to humanity lies in working in our local environment. Only by concerted prayer can we have a wider influence on the world's progress, while the witness of our lives produces results on those immediately around us. Each kindly action changes the perspectives of those in contact with us, and so starts a chain reaction that culminates in a change of heart of many people.

The work is slow and the immediate rewards meagre, but it is thus that the Holy Spirit guides people towards a greater understanding of the world in which they live.

But what of the psychic field to which I have referred, in passing, several times? Are we not living in times when many are turning to the area of the psychic for help? It is very important that those seeking the spiritual path should know how the psychic faculty relates to it.

CHAPTER 13

The psychic faculty and the spiritual path

AS THE PERSONALITY BECOMES better integrated, so the soul within it makes its presence known ever more strongly. It becomes more articulate as we advance to the inner silence where the voice of God is heard. But in this silence other impressions enter our awareness also. These are from the extrasensory world that interpenetrates our own material one. In it float the fears and desires, the dejection and the aspiration, of all those in contact with us, and also those who have passed into the greater life beyond the grave. The soul's eloquence is touched by the urgency of psychical communication, and the personality is very liable to be overwhelmed by this influx of extrasensory information which comes to it from the unconscious reaches of the mind. Such a personality may easily lose its balance unless the origin and validity of psychic communication is pondered on with care and compassion.

The fact of extrasensory sources of communication is not treated kindly by materialistically inclined intellectuals, who would confine all forms of communication to the tangible five senses of the body. Yet in all relationships it is the unspoken word that makes the deepest impression, and the unenunciated impression that lasts longest. As we become more attentive to the silence round us, so other modes of apprehension make themselves known to us.

The feature that these impressions have in common is their circumscribed area of influence. In other words, they are strictly personal in character. They speak directly to us as persons, sometimes enhancing our own opinion of ourselves, but often broadening the scope of our understanding by bringing to our awareness new modalities of existence. Sometimes these sources of communication have a demonic character, instilling a fanatical sectarianism into the recipient of the information, and interfering more and more with the conduct of his life. In all, the psychic realm is one of transition from the solid stability of the earth to the eternal presence of the spiritual life.

Much of the psychic side of life emanates from dark forces in our own unconscious minds and those of other minds around us. It is quite probable that certain mentally ill people are unusually receptive to psychic influences, but because of their poor powers of discernment, they are unable to comprehend the source of the communication or evaluate its significance. Various drugs used for gaining psychedelic experiences may have a similar effect. Let us consider some of the manifestations of the psychic field.

The first point to be made is that *the soul is the organ of both psychical information and spiritual enlightenment.* The more active the reasoning mind, or intellect, the more are psychic impressions excluded. On the other hand, those who are not subservient to the intellect, whose minds are still and attentive, will be aware of greater psychic communication from those round them, and finally even from the world beyond the grave. If survival of death is to be a reality for us, we need to acquire the stillness within so that the departed may speak directly to us. If our relationships with those still alive in the flesh are real, so likewise will we come to know of their dispositions long before they confide them to us. The psychic realm is particularly tractable to primitive races who have not as yet developed the reasoning side of the mind sufficiently to exclude ubiquitous psychic impressions. Such people can, in their primitive way, live in passionate harmony with their surroundings, even the climatic ones, and they have much to teach us about communion with nature. Their souls are ardent but their personality is integrated on such a humble level of performance that they are incapable of embracing a view of humanity wider than that of their immediate surroundings. The reasoning mind is both the censor of impressions reaching the consciousness from outside and the co-ordinator of these impressions, so that they become fashioned into a coherent body of knowledge.

The intellect is naturally suspicious of those intangible modalities of existence which it cannot immediately dominate. If it is left in charge of the whole personality, it will suppress and deny anything that it cannot understand. This dominance of the intellect is both a feature of our contemporary scientific way of life, and a source of bitter denunciation by various irrational groups that flourish as a protest against the desiccating power of pure reason. Neither point of view has, in my opinion, the whole truth. If the intellect is in total command of the personality, the result is a truncation of the full man. The emotional, or feeling, response to reality is played down, and all thoughts or ideas that cannot be accurately measured or proved experimentally are derided and dismissed from consciousness.

Of course, the emotional nature with its strong psychic undertones cannot be quenched as easily as this, and it makes its presence felt in outbursts of irrational behaviour that mar the calm façade that the intellectual person presents to the world. We cannot, in other words, insulate ourselves against the onslaught of psychic impressions. It is particularly unfortunate that the church as a whole is still opposed to the psychic dimension of reality. While it should be rightly suspicious of many psychic manifestations, it should also practise the gift of discernment of spirits so that it can teach its flock what is good and what is questionable. A blanket denunciation of psychism is a terrible error, and one which in its turn can lead to the excesses of witch-burning and other atrocities against those who possess psychic gifts.

Nevertheless, irrational groups of people who are guided by the psychic sense without using the reason as a censor also cause much harm. The danger is not so much that of being taken over by evil, demonic forces, though these certainly exist and can cause dangerous obsession in people especially open to the influence of unseen powers because of their own weak will. The real danger is that the power of free choice, which is the essence of the will, is gradually stolen from the person who comes to rely increasingly on irrational occult forces.

The flight from reason in our own century is one of the most terrible manifestations of the power of demonic possession. It was seen in its full flower in Hitlerite Nazism, but the many groups now practising occultism are in a similar danger. Once the reason is totally abdicated, man becomes the victim, indeed the repository, of dark forces that arise within him but originate as part of a psychic residue of evil that has accumulated from the beginning of time through the selfish abuse of free will by sentient creatures. And do not let us limit these only to human forms. The angelic hierarchy, an object of derision amongst materialists, is real enough to those with powers of seership—and the angels are very different from the winged creatures depicted in popular paintings! As man becomes fully himself, he begins to have some greater conception of the magnitude of the world he inhabits! The astronomers are amazing us with one aspect of the vastness of the universe, but it is to the psychologists and especially to the mystics that we must turn for other insights into the meaning of reality. Again I stress that none of this is to be taken on trust. Until such time as it is shown directly to us, an attitude of courteous agnosticism is mandatory. Always hold on to reason, but never let it dictate the nature of truth. Its function is to assess new insights, and if these are acceptable, to bring them into harmony with past knowledge so that a new synthesis may be effected.

How can one test the validity of psychic impressions? By the nature of the communication, the personality of the communicator, and above all by the effect the impression makes on the aspirant. "By their fruits ye shall know them" is the acid test. The fruits of undeveloped psychism are seldom very attractive. The psychic ability usually boosts the personality of those who have it, leading to a dangerous psychic inflation, which is one form of spiritual pride. There is a temptation to meddle in the lives of other people, to read their thoughts, and to sit in judgment over them. All this stresses once more the very personal nature of psychic communication, whether between two friends in the flesh or between a discarnate source and an aspirant still on earth. The distressingly low level of spirituality that one so often finds in spiritualistic groups is an indication that the psychic way is not necessarily superior in spiritual worth to the sensory way of communication that we use from day to day.

The gifts of the spirit

There is another, much more attractive aspect of psychism. This is the increased psychic sensitivity that develops in those who are on the spiritual path, the path beyond self-gratification

to self-sacrifice for the love of man and God. As one progresses
in the way of the spirit, so the gifts of the Spirit are bestowed on
one. This way is usually far less spectacular than the rather
dramatic downpouring of the Holy Spirit that occurs in the
pentecostal experience, but in my opinion, is of considerably
greater profundity and worth. The danger of a dramatic experience, especially in a group whose religious emotions have been
stirred up into a vortex of enthusiasm by the techniques of reviva-
lism, is that it tends to exalt the personality. The person in
question feels he has arrived, and is spiritually superior to those
who have not been similarly initiated! This is one of the great
criticisms of the psychism found in immature people. It boosts
their personal self so that it becomes inflated and masquerades
as the soul, or spiritual self. On the other hand, the psychism that
develops as a part of the integration of the personality is unobtrusive, fleeting initially but eventually becoming more constant,
and is not concerned with boosting the personality of the aspirant.
In fact, it quickens his understanding of and compassion for
other people, whose need he feels before they have had time to
utter it.

Such psychism is purposeful. It does not impinge on the
consciousness simply to make its presence felt. It comes to us,
on the contrary, to direct us into a positive response to some outer
circumstance. This is the type of communication that may start
between husband and wife, or between those very close in friendship. The most authentic mode of communication is by thought
—or mental telepathy. This comes unheralded and in perfect
lucidity as a message entering the head. Its invasion of the silence
is usually so abrupt and decisive that your whole trend of
thought is disrupted and a new direction of thinking is thrust on
you. Alternatively, a transmitted value judgment may arrive in
one's awareness as a feeling, exhilarating or sickening as the case
may be, in the region of the solar plexus. Those who are psychically attuned learn to pay attention to these indications of communication from others round them. The proof lies in the rapid
confirmation of the material transmitted by an occurrence on a
worldly level. This in a strange way substantiates the purpose-
fulness of the impression vouchsafed psychically. In other words,
the psychism of the spiritually advancing person is well planned
by the active soul, has a clear purpose, and does not boost his
personality. There may also be shafts of clairvoyance in which

features of another's true nature are revealed in terms of an external emanation of radiance, called an "aura". And even the past and future may to some extent be laid bare so that some of their contents are glimpsed. All this emphasises that the true being, or soul, lies outside the limitation of time and space, while being directly enmeshed in it through its connexion with the body and the reasoning mind.

Spiritual directors warn their disciples against the psychical path because, in itself, it is as much a dead end as is naked materialism. The lower psychic powers, or "siddhis" as they are called in the East, have much glamour attached to them. And by the use of them the occultist can gain power over both the material world and the lives of other people. Apart from the disastrous effect that such power has on its objects, it destroys the practitioner even more completely, for abused power separates the subject from the world around him. Occultism is to be thought of as the study and use of psychic powers, both receptive and executive, to gain greater understanding of one's environment, including other people. When seen in this context, the term is divested of some of its invidious associations. Its occult nature is related to the hidden aspects of the world—hidden, that is, from the spiritually blind individual—and does not necessarily indicate secrecy. But the difficulty lies in human nature which is very likely to seize occult knowledge for personal gain. It is very doubtful whether practitioners of occultism ever achieve happiness personally or bestow happiness on others. The occult path comes once again to a dead end.

St. Paul speaks eloquently about this: "And though I have the gift of prophecy, and understand all mysteries, and all knowledge; and though I have all faith, so that I could remove mountains, and have not charity, I am nothing." It is the superimposition of power, without love, on knowledge that renders psychism and occultism a dead thing. But if the spiritual nature is in control, the psychic faculty blossoms into increasing beauty and much of what is "occult" to the world at large becomes open to the seer.

It is therefore right to regard the psychic sense as a natural human faculty usually best developed in quiet, unintellectual people. In itself it can be a very useful adjunct to the personality so long as it does not get out of hand or inflate the person's self-esteem. But it is never infallible. At times it is remarkably accurate, but on other occasions it fails miserably. To disregard it is foolish, but to rely on it absolutely is disastrous. It is in the deeper part of the soul, where the spirit lies, that truth may be known, but such knowledge of truth is not a function of the psychic faculty any more than it is one of the unaided intellect. The psychic faculty is unreliable because it is closely attached to the emotions, which are a notoriously bad guide to action or the discernment of truth. The prejudgment, or prejudice, that is an inevitable part of our emotional response to people and things will attach itself to the psychic faculty and pervert it. This is why mediumship is full of pitfalls and is so unsatisfactory in bringing down to earth really important inspirational material. The great creators of the race have always worked on a higher level of reality than the crudely psychic.

Nevertheless, the psychic sense is not to be deprecated. It is our first intimation of a realm of unspoken reality that lies beyond the solid earth on which we set our feet. Many people are jolted unceremoniously out of naïve positivism, whether humanistic or traditionally religious, by a sudden opening of their psychic faculties. A convincing experience of mental telepathy may be talked away as mere coincidence by the compulsive sceptic, but the person who has had the experience is left questioning the nature of reality, and he will seek an answer in the future course of his life. Even more impressive is the not uncommon out-of-the-body experience, when the conscious part of the personality is so detached from the body that it can look down upon it and see it lying inertly below. On some occasions the focus of consciousness, which is in fact the soul, can move beyond the limitation of the body and travel some distance away from it, and confirm the experience by bringing back verifiable information. Cases of this type are well recorded in the annals of psychical research. Furthermore, the disembodied soul can on occasions penetrate realms of existence that are not of this earth at all, but are part of the greater life of the world to come in which the departed may be encountered. And on rare occasions a realm of light devoid of all objects of sensation may be attained. This is the state of transcendent meaning and is the realm of the mystic. There are then gradations from the trivialities of much mundane psychic communication to the world-transcending vista of the mystic. All are psychically mediated—by which I mean that the communication is mediated through the soul with recourse to sensory substantiation. All teach us of the reality of the soul, which is the very centre of the personality and its fixed point. All convey the basic realisation of the unity of life that transcends all divisions and brings the divided parts home in a new synthesis. We are indeed all members one of another. It is the psychic sense that confirms this fundamental truth. Without this understanding we would be eternally fighting to preserve and enhance our own lives at the expense of the greater body of mankind. No one who is psychically aware can doubt the close communion that exists between men, and potentially between man and the kingdom of nature.

It may be asked why if the psychic sense is as real as I have portrayed it, scientific investigations into the paranormal have yielded such equivocal data. It seems clear that the type of attitude necessary for psychic sensitivity to blossom is not easily cultivated in research laboratories, supervised quite often by compulsive sceptics who are, at least unconsciously, determined to explode the myth of psychic awareness. This hostile attitude, or even a coldly detached one, cannot but detract from the performance of any psychically sensitive person (indeed called a "sensitive", or more contentiously a "medium"). In psychic work the harder one tries, the more certain is one to fail in the task. This is because the reason forces itself to the helm of conscious personality and is determined to take charge, even to the extent of producing data that transcend the reason! It is in quiet relaxation and trusting tranquillity that psychic communication is most likely to penetrate the clear untroubled mind. As soon as the personal self takes charge, it looks for results which will enhance its own prestige.

It is fortunate indeed that the psychic sense is not under the direct control of the selfish will, although occultists have tried hard throughout the ages to render psychism subservient to their drive for power. This whole question of the will and the spiritual life needs great clarification, and it is therefore appropriate that we should now examine its nature and function in our approach to God.

CHAPTER 14

Freedom and the will

THERE IS NO MORE important factor in the spiritual life than an actively functioning will. And yet often in psychological and religious circles the concept of will is regarded either with derision or with distrust. The modern schools of psychology, the behaviouristic and the psychodynamic, are sceptical, to say the least, of the very existence of a will sufficient to enable the person to become a free agent. Traditional religionists, on the other hand, confuse the will with wilfulness. To them the will means the will to power, to self-assertiveness, to lordship over the world, and as such it is directly opposed to God's will. Therefore they believe that the spiritual man must abdicate his own will altogether and make himself subject to God's will.

If only the latter were easily ascertainable this advice might be quite acceptable! Unfortunately, as we have already seen, there is no divine oracle at hand, nor do the world's sacred scriptures give a completely coherent doctrine, to say nothing of the fact that they were written centuries ago and often have little direct advice to give as regards the peculiar problems that confront a scientifically orientated world. If there is some abiding meaning to our lives we have to accept personal responsibility for our conduct. Whatever the theoreticians may say, we have to accept the fact of will as a part of our life in the world.

It is instructive, therefore, to ponder the psychological objections to the concept of will, for they are by no means foolish, and indeed have much truth in them. To the behaviourist, the actions of a person derive from his past responses to various stimuli reaching his brain. The concept of mind apart from the activity of the brain is not accepted by this important school of psychologists. Thus while new stimuli can evoke different patterns of behaviour, the person himself is in no way in command of the response. Such a view of personality is important in that it emphasises the role that conditioned reflexes play in our behaviour, but it cannot account for the finer aspects of personality, the aspects that speak of the uniqueness of human nature.

To the psychodynamic school of psychologists, who adhere to the theories of Freud and his successors, the importance of the unconscious mind is stressed, and rightly so. It is the repository of many drives that are only fitfully brought into conscious awareness, and indeed some are permanently submerged. But they come to consciousness when the "censor" is removed. This occurs during dreams and also in various situations when we are taken off our guard. The influence of the drives is, however, more subtle than this. They pervade all our conscious actions and are the real source of our attitudes. Freud, of course, stressed the pre-eminence of sex, in the broadest context, as the motivator of our conscious actions, but others have also drawn attention to the will to power and to the will to survive. Now all these unconscious impulses are very important in the conduct of our lives, and we are indebted in no small measure to the insights and understanding of these pioneers of modern psychology who have laid bare the motivation of much allegedly altruistic and religious activity. I need not emphasise that much religious observance, particularly in the past, was based more on the fear of divine retribution than on the love of God. Likewise a conventional churchgoer could trade on the esteem of his neighbours for his piety, whereas a candid agnostic would arouse the suspicion and hostility of those around him. Nor can the repressed sexual undertones of some types of religious ritual be denied. Some of the greatest mystics have used erotic imagery to symbolise the union of man and God, thereby reinforcing the belief of agnostic psychologists that the life of the cloister, by repressing normal sexuality, stimulated orgiastic yearnings.

There can be no doubt that much of what passes for a strong free will in a successful person is often, in reality, an unconscious drive moving the person in a predetermined pattern of response. For instance, one who has suffered from rejection or material insecurity as a child may be so dominated by a desire for safety and esteem that his whole life is devoted to making money or acquiring power over other people. On the surface we may admire the single-tracked will power that has made such material success possible, but in fact the individual himself is little more than a small child in possession of great riches with which he can defend himself against the onslaughts of the inhospitable world. A life devoted to the achievement of a circumscribed material ambition at the expense of a full development of the personality cannot be regarded as satisfactory, no matter how "successful" it may appear on the surface.

This, of course, does not mean that all materially successful people are inadequate and immature. Their degree of maturity does, however, depend not merely on their success in any one particular enterprise but in the wider field of relationships with other people and their attitude to the world and to life itself. "What shall it profit a man if he shall gain the whole world and lose his own soul?" asks Jesus. A person driven by unconscious impulses does not know himself at all, but merely identifies himself with the particular drive that has possessed all his psychic energy. Thus a great deal of the will is really not free at all, but is bound to unconscious desires that dominate the personality. No wonder many psychologists are sceptical about the concept of will, at least in a context of freedom and responsibility.

The freed will

However there is still more to be said about the will than this. There are times when it is a conscious activity derived not from hidden drives but from the deep desire to find meaning in the dark world we inhabit. Desire is the stimulus that sets the will in action. Where there is no desire, there is no action whatsoever and the person lies inert. Desire is often deprecated in religious circles, but without it there would be no growth into the knowledge of God. Desire for purely personal gratification or for self-aggrandisement, even to the extent of gaining personal knowledge of divine things, leads to disillusionment and despair. But a desire for the good of others besides ourselves, a desire which is the prerequisite for the action of love, is the way of true understanding of the self. And this desire sets in motion the spiritual quest, a quest not to be fully realised in this life, but one that leads us out of the darkness of selfish isolation into the ever increasing light of fellowship with others.

It follows then that the will is the active response of the

personality to the various desires to which it is heir. The flesh
has its desires of survival, nourishment, and sexual satisfaction
which are so inveterate that they manifest themselves continually
as the unconscious drives we share in common with the animal
creation. In the case of many people the will is identified with
the satisfaction of these primitive drives, and there is no freedom
of action outside the body's demands. But in other, more evolved,
people there is an awareness of the world they inhabit, of the
basically incomplete nature of man, and a deeply felt yearning
for understanding and self-fulfilment. It is this desire for
meaning and self-realisation, often precipitated, as we have
already seen, by some tragedy or great suffering, that leads
us on to the spiritual path, for then at last we realise that, in the
end, nothing matters except the unitive knowledge that comes
from the encounter with God. The true identity of the person,
the soul, now comes into its own. It directs the personality and
indeed eventually so penetrates and pervades the personality that
it becomes soul-filled. At this stage there is an integration of the
body and the mind (with its reasoning and emotional faculties)
under the control of the soul which in turn is directed by the
Spirit of God within it. The controlling, directing action of the
soul is that aspect of the will which is conscious and free.

The freedom of which I speak is a freedom from enslavement
to the senses or the outside environment. It does not cast off the
needs of the body or the directions of the senses any more than
it escapes from being involved in the outside world. But instead
of being subject to these influences, it is in control of them and
gives them that rein which is necessary for the well-being of
the person's physical, emotional, and intellectual faculties without allowing them to take charge and disrupt his personality. Only
when one has established one's identity in a crisis of moral choice
can one really know what is meant by free will. Only then is one
a free agent.

Let us consider some of the attributes of this liberty to be
oneself.

The glory of a freed will—one under the direction of the soul
—is that it can be used for the final flowering of the personality.
It is no longer subservient to the drives of the body and no longer
under the domination of the outside world, being driven hither
and thither by the flux of circumstances. It can act according to

the direction of the Spirit within, and does not need to placate
or bribe other people. Such a will is not, as I have already pointed
out, above the influence of our inner drives or the demands of
the environment around us. It is, on the contrary, very sensitive
to these facts of life, but is no longer subject to them. A free
person is one who can be himself in any situation. He does not
depend on the support of others to sustain his own inner life.
He is not bound by the opinions of others nor the fleeting fortunes
of the world around him. He does not need the patronage of those
whom the world calls great, because his support comes from within him. But being no longer beholden to others, he is an inevitable
centre of attraction and support for them, because in him they
see something, albeit inchoate, of the nature of God. The more
one seeks friends, the more friendless and alone one is. The more
the kingdom of God, which is within us and around us, is sought,
the more will all other things, and above all, loving human relationships, be added to us. This is *the law of spiritual supply*. It
is clear that, at this stage of being, the will is no longer a thrust-
ing assertive force, but is rather the quietening influence in the
personality which makes us receptive to the inner voice. "Be
still, and know that I am God." (Psalm 46.10). It is now that
we can begin to fathom the mystical juxtaposition of the free
will and the will of God.

The free will does not go into a state of restful oblivion and
wait for God to do everything. This error, which is called quiet-
ism, leads to a complete atrophy, or withering, of the personality.
The free will brings the personality under the direction of the
receptive soul, so that the inner voice can make its wordless
message felt. And this message is one of strengthening, for indeed,
it is the Comforter (the bringer of strength) Who is the Holy
Spirit. It is something of a paradox that the person convulsed
with incessant activities is, far from being an active agent, really
passive and under the domination of powerful unconscious drives.
On the other hand, the quiet receptive person who waits patiently
on the Spirit is showing great inner activity.

Contemplation is the most exalted activity that man can perform. In it the whole personality is, under the action of the
enlightened will, kept quiet so that the Holy Spirit can inspire it
and lead it into greater truth. This apparently simple action of
the will takes a longer time to fulfil than we could bear to consider.
It is the very meaning and purpose of life. It is the core of the

great statement of Jesus, "For whosoever will save his life shall lose it, but whosoever shall lose his life for my sake and the gospel's the same shall save it." (St. Matthew 16.25). Indeed, the life that is saved is no longer the circumscribed life of the personality but the all-pervading consciousness of the soul that extends to the nethermost regions psychically and mystically.

Thus the *end of the spiritual life is liberty*. Liberty is quite different from licence, in which there is no imposed control on the drives and lusts of the body and mind and the person is free to do whatever he likes. The end of licence is disintegration of the personality and the collapse of the social order, because if there is no higher direction, the animal selfishness that is part of our earthly inheritance will dominate our lives. Real freedom is far from being a condition in which we are in absolute charge of ourselves according to the personal selfishness we exhibit. It is a state of willed discipline to the highest we know, a knowledge that is innate in the soul, and which, through the gift of faith, is made manifest in our lives. St. Paul describes himself as a servant of Jesus Christ, and yet it was through the same Christ that he passed beyond the bondage of the law to the love in which all law is consummated. This love is no instant attainment. It requires a life consecrated in ardour and self-giving to the highest we know for love to dawn upon us and transform us. It is in such service only that there is perfect freedom. The way to this heavenly freedom is by the enlightened will, a will free from all carnal and intellectual encumbrances, yet at the same time glorifying the body and the mind.

Discipline and the spiritual life

The proper use of the will is the basis of discipline. In the early stages of the ascent to God we should have the desire to serve Him sufficiently to be prepared to give of a little of our time to worship Him. Thus the will must be active enough to cause us to retire from the work in which we are engaged, whatever it is, and move to God in silent meditation. This is one of the reasons why time set aside assiduously for the inner life is an essential part of our spiritual development. In the religious life, the Office is recited to bring the mind to recollectedness. In the early stages of prayer, the mind may derive great benefit from the willed visualisation of sacred scenes, parables, and symbols. Later

it often becomes fatigued, bored, and apparently far from th
awareness of the divine reality. Then it is that the will should lea
the mind into greater stillness, so that beyond even the range o
the discursive intellect, a realm of ineffable reality may be touche
where the soul is enraptured in the silence, and worships th
eternal Godhead in wordless adoration.

Discipline is the way in which the components of the person
ality are put progressively under the direction of the spirit tha
is the highest part of the soul. If the will acts in this way ther
is a sacrifice of the personal self that is necessary for the emer
gence of the spiritual self, or soul. When the personality is infuse
by the authenticity of the soul, the will is free and acting unde
the direct instructions of the Holy Spirit. Then we are indee
participants in God's will. In St. Augustine's famous dictum
"Love, and do what you will," we see the meaning of a free
will. In real love, as I said earlier, the centre of our being is n
longer rooted in the personal self but in the soul, which is i
eternal communion, through the spirit, with all other souls an
with God. Love seeks not its own but rather the liberty tha
embraces all the children of God. Thus when we know of thi
transcendent, and yet impersonal, love, we are free, and what
ever we do is to God's greater glory.

This is man's end—to worship God and to enjoy Him forever
Our will is most closely attuned to His will when we are mos
like what He was when He became flesh of our flesh. In th
incarnation of Christ we see the coincidence of the human and th
divine wills, separate yet united. And this is the promise for a
mankind as it partakes fully of the divine nature deeply ingraine
in it, yet sadly obscured by a perverse will. We have to grow
into a knowledge of God through faith and an enlightened will

The will can never force a knowledge of God. It is importan
to recognise that. Even the most exhaustive techniques of medi
tation that aim at forcing open the very doors of heaven an
bringing us face to face with God Himself fail miserably. Thei
fruits are illusory psychical phenomena, not the peace that passe
understanding—that peace which Jesus left with His disciples
the peace He gave them which was so unlike the trivial peace o
the world. For power, whether secular or occult, there is grea
striving. For the peace of God there is only submission and self
sacrifice. And yet everything that is surrendered and sacrifice
is restored, blessed in name and transfigured in essence. Th

freed will, which shows itself in real personal protest against moral evil at the beginning of its ministry, fulfils itself by making the personality receptive to the love of God. A freed will is therefore necessary for God's grace to be properly received and perfectly used. We shall return to God from Whom we come as free agents. The will is the power behind the action of return. And we shall return as mature, integrated human beings full of the knowledge of the love of God. Every consciously willed act in God's name (or nature) leads us to the moment of union with Him.

Mysticism at its peak is that union with the Divine. Let us think about mysticism and spirituality, with this in mind.

CHAPTER 15

Mysticism and spirituality

INTERPENETRATING AND TRANSCENDING THE world of phenomenal life there is an order of being that both sustains life and draws it to its final destination. The order of being of which I speak is all-embracing, having no finite parts, and neither beginning nor end. It embraces every created object. Indeed, the validity of the identity of any object, whether material or personal, lies in its belonging to this greater scheme of reality. This reality is as far above the personal as the personal exceeds the physical, and yet each object is sustained as itself in and by the all-embracing reality. In other words, the unique identity of each person (and created object) is never impugned or obliterated. On the contrary, it is confirmed and glorified in the eternal presence of which it is both an integral part and a universal whole.

This is the experience of mysticism, and to any who have been given it (for it never comes entire by willed assertiveness from the personality) by the grace of God, a new understanding both of the meaning of life and the nature of God dawns upon consciousness. It is no wonder that mystical experience is sought above all else by those who know, for in the glimpse of reality vouchsafed, the meaning and destiny of individual existence is dimly comprehended. However, both the experience and the effect its advent has on the subsequent life of the aspirant need careful consideration, for not every self-transcending experience is truly mystical, and indeed certain episodes of this type may be associated as much with brain dysfunction as with spiritual growth. Although the great mystics of the world have transformed the nature of society and man's view of reality by their ministry and teaching, it is nevertheless true that groups which have indulged heavily in practices that lead to dissociation of the personality have all too often tended to ignore the physical and social side of life. And drug-induced mystical states are not infrequently the precursors of a serious disintegration of the personality, so much so that the word mysticism is equated in many minds with irrational behaviour, occult tendencies, and a general inability to face the realities of everyday life. All these accusations have unfortunately a certain truth in them, and yet the true mystic is the most exalted of men, for he has seen the light of reality, and has been illuminated by it.

The true mystical experience, though rare in its full expression, is not at all uncommon in those whose personalities are becoming better integrated, and who are living constructively and creatively in the society where they belong. The characteristic feature of a mystical experience (or a "peak experience" as it is more usually called by humanistic psychologists) is *an awareness of union*. The distance that separates subject and object in discursive meditation or in everyday relationships is suddenly, for a brief spell of time, transcended, and in that moment the identity of the person expands to embrace the identity of the object. In fact the soul is being explored. As Heraclitus said some 2,500 years ago; "You can never find out the boundaries of the soul, so deep are they." It is in the most sacred part of the soul, the spirit, that God reveals Himself to us. In the soul the barriers of time are dissolved and a state of eternity prevails. Eternity is not an endlessly long period of time, as the mathematician would define it, but rather the totality of being to which nothing, whether time or space, can be added. It is in this eternity that God is known, not by direct revelation, for It (as the Godhead) is outside the scope of rational cognition, being the eternal void from which all creation moves. In It is the eternal generation of the Trinity: creator Father, uncreated Son by Whom all substantive creation is evoked as the word of God, and the Spirit that effects creation and infuses all created things with life that brings them through willed action (in a time-space world) back to the Father as responsible agents.

In mystical experience the Godhead reveals Itself by its outpouring energies. Of these two are pre-eminent—love and light. The love that bears the creature, as it were in the everlasting arms, is personal in regard to the creature—who is a person—

but also beyond personality in regard to the whole cosmos. The cosmic dimension of divine love is transpersonal, but never impersonal. Transpersonal love never denies the unique nature of any creature, but loves all creatures equally without respect of their uniqueness. The mystic glimpses in his vision the mind of Christ, and all mystics, of whatever religious tradition or none, are in the mind of the cosmic Christ when they are illuminated. This mind is one of light, not created, but an overflowing energy of God. Its intensity is such that it illuminates every part of the created universe. Its illumination is physical, in that it blinds the bodily eye by its radiance, psychical in that it illuminates the world of soul relationship by the experience of union and reconciliation, and intellectual, in that it reveals to the heightened reason the purpose, meaning, and end of individual life.

It is no wonder that Christ is described as "God of God, light of light, very God of very God" in the Nicene Creed. This is no symbolic statement. It is an affirmation of the indescribable radiance of uncreated light which is also the light of transfiguration. An illuminated person is physically transfigured, and this transmutation of the flesh and the mind should proceed even when the experience is but a past memory. The soul is also aware of a harmony so perfect that it resembles music of no earthly type. It has been called the music of the spheres; unlike the music of this world it is continuous and undivided. Of course, this is an impossible situation in terms of the music heard by the body's ear, which depends for its effect on its time sequences. But the celestial music is the source of all earthly music, transcribed in time sequence by the reasoning mind.

The intellectual illumination that accrues from mystical experience is spontaneous. It is a primary intimation and does not follow intellectual analysis. On the contrary, the ratiocination that brings the mystical revelation into a new metaphysic follows the experience and is the fruit of later discursive meditation. For every aspect of mysticism is an extension of the well-recognised facts of reality. The radiance of the uncreated light is also the void which is eternally dark and obscure. The harmony of the uncreated sound is heard in complete silence. The love that embraces all creation in the flow of life is felt without personal touch. It therefore follows that, in mysticism, there is an inevitable reconciliation between apparently irreconcilable opposites. It is thus that that the mystic is the leader of men towards a broader synthesis in which sects flow into the universal church, and science finds its ultimate source and end in spiritual reality.

The facts of mystical illumination are *the eternity of life* and *the forgiveness of sins*. It is in illumination that the very relative role of the physical body in the life of the person is understood. The soul stands outside the time sequence, and is immortal according to the love of God who created it. But the body is not merely an unimportant physical covering that is to be discarded when death occurs. On the contrary, it is to be resurrected in spiritual reality. Thus the building of the spiritual body is the most important personal work that has to be performed when the soul is in incarnation.

The forgiveness of sin follows the ineffable love that comes to us from God. This forgiveness is unconditional, being an inevitable result of love. To be forgiven requires only the submission of self in complete faith to the power of God, and then a change in heart, in mind, and in strength is given one. We earn forgiveness, not by a positive act of selfish will trying to elevate ourselves to the divine reality of good works, but by accepting the unconditional love of God. If the atoning sacrifice of Jesus could be seen as a material demonstration of this mystical fact, the redemption of the personality that His act made possible would be better understood. Forgiveness leaves the person free to continue his path towards full integration of the personality. He is no longer hindered or sidetracked by the thought of revenge or the emotion of guilt that prevents him in his real work, which is integration and self-realisation. Indeed, in the experience of mysticism he is given a preview, in a mere flash of time, of what he and the whole world are to become when the spirit is fully revealed in the soul. This is the knowledge of fulfilment, whose height is love.

It follows from all this that *the hall-mark of real mysticism is intuitive knowledge*. A mystical experience is not simply a marvellous feeling or an emotional release. While these components are surely present, they are secondary events. It is the opening of the mind into a new way of understanding that is the real criterion of mystical illumination. This higher understanding is called "gnosis". It speaks of the eternity of life, the reality of a spiritual order that governs and sustains the physical order (which is in fact a reflection of the spiritual, and not to be thought of as basically separate or even different from the one reality that is spiritual), and the fact of God, Who is beyond all categories of thought but Who reveals Himself to His creatures as personal love and is seen in the cosmos as transpersonal love, uncreated energy, and preordained purpose. The mystic knows, but is not a "gnostic" in the limited, exclusive sense of that ill-used word. He knows he is not one of the "elect" who has been chosen to form a group in which to guard the "mysteries" (of which there are none, for everything of God is open and universal according to the person's ability to receive and comprehend). On the other hand, he returns to the world as he was before his illumination —simple, quiet, unobtrusive, and yet inwardly transformed by the experience of eternity he has had. What he is radiates from him in greater work, service, and healing to those around him.

As regards forgiveness, remember always that the redemption that follows the acceptance of God's love does not automatically make one perfect. This requires a long path of discipline using the free will and acting upon the grace of God. Whatsoever a man sows, that shall he surely reap is the law of life. It is called "karma" in the East. But karma is redeemed by the love of Christ. Its emotional energies are transformed, ceasing to be destructive and repetitive. Thus a redeemed karma is worked out in love and joyful anticipation, not in fear of future consequences or in a spirit of revenge. Even worldly punishment or bodily suffering is transfigured so that each experience loses its threat and becomes a stepping-stone towards the integration of the personality. In this way our wounds become as worships before God, to recall Dame Julian's words again. The path towards spiritual realisation is strait and narrow, but it is not uphill. The narrowness is a manifestation of its essential balance, the middle way of Buddhism.

Incomplete manifestations of mysticism

The unitive experience occurs as a milestone on the spiritual path. Far from being the end of the journey, it is a confirmation by God's grace that all one has stored in one's faith is a living reality. It comes like the wind, blowing as it will, so that no one can tell where it comes from or where it is to go. This is the way of the Holy Spirit. I do not believe that anyone who is on the path of discipleship is left without an experience of union of God with the created universe, but there are all grades from the fully manifested experience which is known to the great mystics of the race to the fleeting peak experiences that lighten the worldly darkness of the humble aspirant. It is not the intensity of the experience that determines its validity, but rather the effect it has on the future life of the disciple. The acid test is (and I make no apology for saying this again): "By their fruits ye shall know them."

This judgment is particularly important nowadays because many people are trying to force the pace of their own inner understanding by the use of drugs that so disturb the working of the brain that material of various hierarchies of significance enters uncensored into their consciousness. Some of this information is, as far as we can be assessed from the descriptions given by drug-takers, similar in quality to the unitive experience of the mystic. Another type of approach that is much in vogue at present is the use of various types of meditation techniques, mostly derived from the Eastern religious tradition, which, by a process of auto-hypnosis through the repetition of mantras, can lay the mind open to the influx of material from sources beyond the physical. While the discipline of meditation is essential for the development of the spiritual will (the free will from the soul), it is only one aspect of the spiritual life. When beginners start indulging in alleged techniques of self-realisation without submitting first to the dedication of all they have and are to God's greater glory and the service of their fellow men, the results are not likely to be helpful to them even if they are able to glimpse mystical reality. It is important to consider the matter in detail.

We live our lives amphibiously between the sensory information of the physical world and the psychic communication of the realm of the soul. In primitive man the reason is so poorly developed that, as I said earlier, psychic impressions invade the personality with little resistance. The result is an animal type of attunement of the person with the environment in which he lives, but free will is so remote that the human dimension of life can scarcely be considered to have begun. As man comes more to himself, the reason develops until it assumes a dominant role. The intellect binds the personality into a coherent unit, but it also separates the person from his environment. Rational man can use his surroundings intelligently for his own benefit, but he cannot lose himself in a self-giving relationship. It is only on the more advanced spiritual path, in which the demands of the self are progressively surrendered in love to the needs of the greater community, that the person moves beyond the thraldom of intellectual dominance and emotional instability to the freedom of the spirit that lightens the soul. At this stage the personality is sufficiently integrated to bear the irruption of mystical information that derives from the spirit, which is of God. But if similar material invades the less developed consciousness of an unspiritual man, the result can be shattering. This happens in its most terrifying form in the course of severe mental illness, when it may disrupt the person's equilibrium entirely and make him feel that he is in direct contact with God. Indeed, he may identify himself with the Almighty.

A not altogether dissimilar result may follow the irruption of mystical material into the consciousness of rather undeveloped people under the influence of hallucinogenic drugs or meditation techniques that cause them to lose their sense of physical identity. Thus not every self-transcending experience is beneficial to the personality. Some such experience may lead to disintegration.

On the other hand, it is not unknown for frankly psychotic people to have beneficial self-transcending experiences. These are not to be dismissed as mere symptoms of insanity, for they may act as an integrating centre around which the smashed personality could reform itself. It is evident that a sane discernment of such events is most important. Only a trained spiritual director can be relied on, for an unsympathetic psychiatrist would certainly dismiss all such experiences as psychotic, whereas an untrained, well-meaning religionist might exalt the phenomenon far above its true value.

It follows from all this that mysticism is most convincing when it occurs in healthy, well-balanced people whose lives are self-actualising (or self-realising), and whose work in the world is creative and self-effacing. Mystical experience that occurs during the course of a psychosis or after the use of drugs lacks the needle-sharp knowledge, or "gnosis", that follows illumination in a healthy person. The reason for this is that the disrupted personality is unable to comprehend and condense the material that flows into it. For the proper assimilation of such intimations a healthy body and mind are essential.

It is this inner balance that distinguishes a real mystic from a mentally abnormal person. The former brings his intimations into worldly action, while the latter escapes into a private realm of self-transcendence while letting the world's demands go un-heeded. It may be necessary to "drop out" of an inimical society for a short period—as many mystically or occultly inclined young people have done in recent years—but in the end there must be a return, so that the character may be strengthened through the inevitable tension between the demands of society and our own intimations of truth. The result of the resolution of this tension is not only an integrated personality but also a transformed society. The Marxist quite rightly declares that man should cease from merely interpreting the world and should instead change it—indeed this is also the meaning of the Christian revela-tion. But transformation can only follow the full development of the personality of each individual, so that he becomes a truly living man. For this to occur there must be a synthesis of mystical illumination that comes from God and progressive social action that comes from enlightened, self-transcending man. Social action based on purely intellectual precepts, no matter how laudable they are in theory, leads to the enslavement of mankind, and not its liberation.

Mysticism in the modern world

If the modern mystic is to be contrasted with his medieval, or pre-scientific, counterpart, the difference must lie, not in his experience or temperament, but in his general view of the world. Pessimists can see no change for the better in the modern world, but those of us with greater perspective should be able to wel-come many of the recent developments in science, medicine, psychology, economics, and sociology. The reality and glory of the physical universe have been further demonstrated by the work of the scientist, and the denial of the body that was so common amongst mystics of past ages is now seen to be an aberration. Self-flagellation, asceticism, and crushing poverty, far from being the way of God, are a repudiation of the theology of creation. When God created the world, He saw that it was all very good.

The spiritual path has been under the closest scrutiny by modern psychologists armed with Freud's destructive criticism of theism. While no unbiased person could accept the finality of the Freudian critique of religion—and indeed some of his later colleagues, especially Jung, have reinstated the religious quest as an essential component of mature adult life—it is nevertheless true that no serious aspirant can afford to be ignorant of the psychic power that drives the personality from its unconscious depths. Techniques of auto-hypnotic meditation no less than starvation through ascetic practices can induce dissociated states of the mind that may culminate in mystical experiences, but the product of these, as has already been noted, is an unbalanced personality. The great saints of the past were able to transcend the harsh circumstances of their lives through the high degree of integration of their personalities. The life of St. Teresa was one in which considerable physical ill-health and nervous strain in her youth were later overcome, so that she became a redoubtable old lady, the reformer of the Carmelite order, and one of the greatest mystics in the Christian tradition. A great modern mystic, Simone Weil, led a life of such asceticism that she died young at a time when her continued witness would have been of great help to the world.

It must be emphasised that mysticism is not only compatible with physical health and a balanced social life, but that the validity of the mystic depends on the contribution he makes both to the society round him in his lifetime and to the spiritual aspiration of subsequent generations. Far from opting out of unpleasant situations, the mystic should be in the forefront leading his fellow-men by the truth of his spiritual vision. When an aspirant falls ill, or becomes the victim of recurrent headaches and other symptoms of physical malaise, he should not submit to this as an act of God or the part he has to play in bearing the sufferings of mankind! He should, according to elementary common sense, check up on his way of life, and try to ascertain where he is going wrong. He may need more rest or a change of scene. Holidays, relaxation, and the simple pleasures of life are as important for the mystic as they are for other people. Likewise good food, clothing, and housing are prerequisites for the spiritual life. If these are denied there will be bodily dysfunction and mental disturbance. In such a person there can be little effective free will.

This leads us to a consideration of the social implications of spirituality. As we have already noted, the spiritual person must be informed about all relevant aspects of modern life. The world will never be the same as it was before the effects of Marx's social criticism manifested themselves. The inseparable relationship of the individual to the society in which he lives can never be denied again. Thus although the Marxist critique of religion as the opium of the people cannot be sustained if we survey the entire personality of man with its innate spiritual aspirations, there can be no permanent withdrawal of the aspirant from the world of relationships into a private retreat where the luxury of spiritual development can be enjoyed in selfish exclusiveness. The spiritual integrity of the mystic is inseparably related to the happiness of his fellows. The phases of withdrawal and return are part of the spiritual life; we withdraw in order to recollect our dependence on God, and we return once more to share this blessing with the world. As I have already said, there can be no effective spiritual aspiration in people who are starved, deprived of medical and social care, or so uneducated that they can scarcely communicate intelligently with their fellows.

It is the tacit acknowledgement of this basic fact that is at the root of social advancement. No country can deny its urgency. No person can be forgotten except to the detriment of everyone else. That we are all members one of another—St. Paul's great mystical insight—is at last being recognised at least on the level of social justice. Much still needs to be done, and the spiritual man can contribute much through his larger, more detached compassion and his ability to reconcile differences in a new synthesis.

The summons to life leads us from a self-centred existence to the encounter with God. But it is we who have to discover the spiritual path.

CHAPTER 16

Discerning the spiritual path

THE PROOF OF SPIRITUAL advancement lies in the altered character of the aspirant. His personality radiates a light—indeed from the uncreated light of God—that illuminates the world around him. Others feel the glow of his presence, not of a powerful dominating person, but as a harbinger of warmth, hope, caring, and faith. No one on the path realises that he is an agent of healing, that his silent presence brings hope and solace to those round him, that his life is a blessing to many. He is far too aware of his shortcomings even to dream that he might be a comfort and support to others. These shortcomings are not the conventional "sins" of popular morality, which in any case has little bearing on our encounter with God. They are the awareness of one's lack of concern at the crucial moment in any relationship. In other words, the truly aspiring person realises continually how much he is lacking in love. Every aspect of the ascent of the personality to God touches this ability to love. The poverty of spirit that is a prerequisite of having the kingdom of heaven is a complete lack of concern for oneself as a separate person, but caring only that one may give oneself adequately (and wisely) for another's healing. It is not an obsessional self-analysis, concerned only with one's own shortcomings and the way of repentance, but rather an ever-present awareness that whatever one does in love for another is always inadequate. It is this humility about the effectiveness of our own efforts that makes us eternally aware of the need for, and the presence of divine grace. There is an innate humility, an inspired simplicity (which has nothing to do with an unworldly naïvety) of the spiritual person that draws others towards him in trust. He speaks not of himself but of the

Holy Spirit that infuses him. And he quite naturally assumes the role of spiritual director. He is not perfect in inspiration. No man can aspire to absolute spiritual knowledge, and indeed the real master of the spiritual life grows in the experience of relationships with the various people who come to him for guidance. Thus there is no sitting on an exalted throne far above the milling masses. Each one, and especially the more dedicated of us, learns by humble service. In the spiritual community the one who is master takes the lowest place. And this applies in life too.

It is the rule that those imbued with great temporal power and wealth are seldom endowed with remarkable spiritual insight. On the other hand, an unnoticed servant may be a spiritual genius. There are mysteries in the destiny of the human personality that are not to be revealed in one brief lifetime on earth.

The fruits of spirituality have been so well enumerated by St. Paul that I can only repeat them : love, joy, peace, longsuffering, gentleness, goodness, faith, meekness, and temperance. It is by these that the calibre of a spiritual man is gauged. I would myself add a tenth : a sense of humour, which is really an extension of the moderation, or balance, that is the secret of temperance. Of all the fruits of divine understanding, a sense of humour is the most mystical, for it sees both the inevitability of contradictory lines of approach to truth, and their resolution, not by conflict or intellectual debate, but in the coincidence of opposites that is at once both ridiculous and sublime. A mystical sense of humour, of which the earthly type is a pale reflection inasmuch as it is personal and restricted, sees that the truth of God is attained by a complete sacrifice of all we hold dear, so that we may know it fully when we no longer possess it in isolation, but are one with it in relationship to all creation. In the Zen tradition a nonsensical riddle is solved by this divine humour that irrupts as a changed awareness into the fixed personality of the disciple.

The antithesis of balance is intensity of purpose. This is so much part of the conventional religious approach that it seems sacrilege to deflate it. In fact, a terrible intensity is not spiritual in direction but personal. The ardent missionary intent on saving the world according to a dogmatic theological scheme is arrogant and humourless. He has so little real faith in God's omnipotence that he believes he has to act as God's deputy. In other words he assumes the divine role and becomes a spiritual dictator, quite unlike God, Who in the person of the Holy Spirit leads the individual through integration to liberty.

The same criticism applies to those who are intense in their dedication to social justice, animal welfare, sexual morality, and many other causes that deserve our full support. For intensity of purpose overrides a love of people, and such a missionary of whatever cause soon becomes an obsessional crank. At this point he betrays the very same cause to which he has dedicated himself, and his fellow men begin to associate the cause with crankiness and imbalance. All too often the essence of truth is discarded with the unpleasant trimmings that surround it. The real error of intensity of purpose lies in an uncertainty about God's being. If we really knew Him we would rest in Him, and He would inspire us to that lightness of action and harmony of response that would effectively achieve the aims that I have mentioned.

The spiritual man changes the world by his spontaneous example, not by impassioned denunciations. He sees the positive side of all situations, no matter how unpleasant they may be, and uses this insight to effect a reconciliation and a change. Reconciliation is not the same as compromise. This is a makeshift agreement without a true resolution of difficulties, and it usually collapses once more into searing conflict. Reconciliation is the construction of a synthesis from conflicting principles, seeing the justice in both sides of the question, and using this insight in resolving the problem. Such reconciliation requires immense love of people and a longsuffering patience that has the inevitable result of being misunderstood by all parties. They can see the agent of reconciliation only as a fence-sitter until their own spiritual vision has been widened by his love. But reconciliation requires a full realisation and admission of sin as well, sin from which no person is exempt, though one is often more guilty than the other. Until there is genuine repentance there can be no reconciliation. This repentance is an opening of oneself to the unconditional love of God in full acknowledgement of past actions. Christ showed the mechanism of this atonement while on earth, and the spiritual man demonstrates its effectiveness by his unconditional love for all the parties in a dispute.

Charismatic gifts

The gifts of the Spirit, enumerated by St. Paul in 1 Corinthians 12, are more exciting than the fruits of the Spirit which he commends in Galatians 5:22. These latter are usually taken for granted—as if they were easily acquired—and it is the gifted ("charismatic") person who is exalted and followed. Of course, the gifts of the Spirit should be a by-product of the spiritual life, and an inevitable outpouring from those who show the fruits of the Spirit. But it is possible to manifest some of the charismatic gifts in the absence of spiritual qualities. This is why the spiritual master is identified not by his unusual powers but by his obvious goodness and love. The power flows as a manifestation of this goodness.

It must be repeated that unspiritual people can possess great psychic gifts. Thus not every gifted "spiritual healer" is a fine person, though the gift of healing is a most important charismatic manifestation. These gifts are psychic, and they tend to inflate the personalities of those who have them. Indeed, a psychic irruption into a spiritually undeveloped person is as likely to have demonic results as divine ones. And unfortunately it is just such a charismatic person who is liable to attract those fresh on the path. A more profound understanding of the gifts of the Spirit is contained in the eleventh chapter of the book of Isaiah in his messianic prophecy (verses 1 to 3): wisdom, understanding, counsel, might, knowledge, and the fear of God, to which is added piety in the Christian tradition. In other words, these gifts of the Spirit lead one to a greater apprehension of the nature of God. Such a knowledge is as far above human cupidity as love is above self-interest. He who is full of the Spirit of God could no more exploit another creature for his own ends than he could seek the praise or approval of another person. It is a matter of perspective. He who has dined at the heavenly table (which is an insight into the nature of the Eucharist when celebrated in mystical awareness) is no longer enraptured by earthly food, but instead seeks to transmute the earthly to the heavenly. The closer one is to the divine source the less important do psychic gifts become. They are as much an encumbrance as material possessions to the spiritually dedicated person. But they cannot be denied; instead they are to be used for the edification of the world, for everything in existence comes from God and is to be brought back to Him redeemed and transfigured.

Of techniques

Our present period is one of intensive spiritual exploration, though this has little contact with the conventional sources of religion. Inasmuch as conventional religion seems more intent in maintaining the status quo and preserving its outer fabric than in exploring the inner world of spiritual reality, it is inevitable that the rising generation should acquire its knowledge of transcendent reality from esoteric, unorthodox sources. That we are on the brink of a "new age" is a commonplace assumption amongst the young of all ages. Judging by the great influx of psychic energy into the world that is manifest not only by cataclysmic political upheavals but also by an increased awareness by many people of the unseen realms of existence, there is considerable substance to this belief. However, it is fatuous to equate this increased psychic sensitivity with spiritual evolution. It could lead (and in view of its cardinal importance I cannot say this too often) to personal disintegration quite as easily as to self-realisation. The forces that are effecting this transformation have to be properly channelled, for they themselves, like all naked power, are ethically neutral. In affluent societies, the harnessing of psychic energy is already one of the more pressing problems at hand, since the age-old struggle for material survival has at last, to a large extent, been overcome by social advancement and a welfare state.

That the ascent of the mind to God cannot be achieved merely by the assertive personal will has already been noted. The grace of God must make the initial movement, but, I repeat, it acts most effectively on a prepared personality. The "preparations" that are in current vogue include those to which I have already referred, the use of drugs that lead to self-transcending experience and various types of meditation techniques. As regards drug-induced experience little can be said in its favour. The real criticism lies not so much in the method, or even in the medical hazards involved in the use of powerful drugs that affect the brain's mechanism, but in the unprogressive nature of the revelation vouchsafed. Even those whose personalities are not disrupted by an unheralded invasion of material from the unconscious part of the mind do not grow in spiritual stature. Instead they rely on the repeated use of the drug to get the same experience, which though no doubt idyllic at its zenith, collapses once more into the divisive state of material existence at its close.

The fruits of psychedelic experience can now be examined dispassionately, for quite a number of years have elapsed since drugs were first introduced into the Western youth culture. These fruits are not impressive; a dropping away from the world is no answer to the problem of its many inadequacies. Since we exist by the work of the society we condemn, we cannot exclude ourselves from it. Eventually we have to return and contribute to it, hopefully to transform it. In other words, drug-induced experiences are at their very best selfish excursions away from the difficulties of the present moment. By their escape from social involvement, they negate the spiritual quest and lead to greater self-centredness.

I would like to add a further word on the current vogue for meditation in the Eastern mode, as it has much more to recommend it. Indeed, one of its greatest achievements has been to release many young people from the thraldom of psychedelic drugs into a world of clearer perception with an intact brain and a more integrated personality. In the last chapter I recorded some misgivings about the loss of physical identity inherent in meditation techniques that use a constantly repeated phrase or mantra. It is common knowledge amongst those engaged in psycho-therapeutic practice and spiritual direction that a certain number of mentally unbalanced people have been involved in meditation of this type. The psychiatric fraternity is therefore generally critical of meditation as a technique. On the other hand, teachers of these techniques, while not denying that some of their students do show signs of mental instability, would argue that the imbalance preceded the technique and would have manifested itself in due course even had the person not practised meditation. Be this as it may, it is nevertheless important to discern beforehand the type of person who should avoid meditation techniques, or else use only those with a strongly discursive element that keeps the mind fully alert.

Certainly the most impressive instances of enhanced spiritual awareness and personal integration that have followed in the wake of these meditation techniques are encountered in the older, more mature person who is already grounded in a religious faith. Thus it is not uncommon for committed Christians to benefit considerably. They acquire an inner strength and balance that is a great help in gaining a deeper understanding of their particular tradition. The emphasis in the Judaeo-Christian tradition is much more on outer action than on the contemplative life. These recently introduced techniques of stilling the mind can help to redress the balance and make the person more integrated around his true self. In the young person, the spiritual value of these types of meditation is much more limited. While he may be weaned off his dependence on drugs by them, the young aspirant is very likely to remain attached to the technique which he regards as the apogee of spiritual knowledge. Indeed, the supercilious arrogance found amongst some of the devotees of idiosyncratic techniques of self-knowledge is unloving and cuts them off from a wider understanding of spiritual reality.

Spiritual experience is a small part of the spiritual life. There are no short cuts in the soul's journey to God. The valleys of suffering are as much a part of the trial as are the mountains of illumination. The validity of a technique lies in the added strength it gives us while we are traversing the arid plains of daily life. In itself it may degenerate into an idol and actually divert us from the vision of God.

Exactly the same criticism must be levelled at some aspects of the charismatic movement. When a person is laid open to what is called the Holy Spirit, he also becomes sensitive to various psychic currents that emanate from his own unconscious mind and the collective unconscious of which Jung speaks. The gift of "speaking in tongues" is not a neurotic manifestation, as its antagonists would assert, but neither is it the last word in prayer. It is a manifestation of a liberated personality articulating its praise to God in a language beyond the bounds of reason. As such it is a liberating experience, but the downflow of psychic energy that may follow this event can lead to severe mental aberration in unbalanced people.

The in-pouring of psychic energies is not a panacea for all ills. If properly channelled and used, they can effect many of the wonderful phenomena described in the Acts of the Apostles, but if they are unleashed on an immature, unbalanced person, they are as likely to cause disintegration as healing. In other words, there is no magical means to salvation, and as I say no short cut to the encounter of man and God. There has to be a progressive growth in the full being of the man before illumination can be fully appreciated and integrated into his personality.

Of far greater value in the spiritual ascent are the well-tried techniques of yoga, which I referred to in an earlier chapter. The way defined by the great spiritual master Patangali is especially helpful. Here the body is given its due place in the scheme of things, and the will is strengthened by the painstaking exercises performed to attain the classical postures. Breathing is acknowledged in its rightful place, and the mind is trained to move beyond discursive thought to that void which is vibrant with life. From this we can learn that a real technique of spiritual advance does not ignore any part of the personality. It develops body and mind, strengthens the will, and liberates the soul. While we should seek to depose the intellect from its seat of crushing domination of the personality, we must never deny its discriminating function. Irrationality is the way to the demonic, and all anti-intellectual philosophies should be eschewed as vigorously as a desiccated intellectualism that denies any mode of being outside the range of the five senses.

The great defect inherent in much Eastern spirituality is the inadequate emphasis laid on grace in the ascent to ultimate reality. This is in part due to the lack of emphasis on the personal nature of God. In the Western theistic tradition the fact of grace is more easily accepted, but a smug reliance on the saving grace of God upon all who "believe" in him (a belief that is usually intellectual and theological rather than existential) all too often leads to spiritual flabbiness. An arrogant assertiveness is usually a façade that hides an inner uncertainty about spiritual reality. What is needed is a synthesis of the classical techniques of Eastern religion with the experience of grace and the infusion of the Holy Spirit that has followed in the wake of the Christian revelation. This synthesis is now being pioneered in some religious houses in the Catholic tradition, and the results are impressive. This is real ecumenism: there is no attempt to deny the differences in emphasis between various traditions or to effect an artificial syncretism. There is instead a deepening understanding of the roots of each tradition, and a union based not on theological manipulations but on the love that follows mystical awareness.

Of course, the various orders in the Roman Catholic Church have their own schemes of spiritual development. The Ignatian Exercises of the Society of Jesus are particularly celebrated, but there are many others also. Nevertheless, these are all specialised and are unlikely to find great currency outside the communities for which they were designed. In any case, their neglect of the development of the whole person—body as well as mind—is unlikely to make them of great interest in the contemporary scene. Nor is the Holy Spirit always allowed leadership in rigidly defined modes of discursive meditation. In another Christian tradition, a meditation based on a deep contemplation of some great sentence from the Bible, so that its essence is distilled from the words that enclose it, is used to bring the mind to an awareness of God, and this can be of great help in integrating the personality.

Each person has to test various techniques to find the one which is true for him. So much depends on our own individuality. This is why we must not be hostile to any movement that releases man from servitude to materialism to an awareness of deeper reality. But the spirit must be tested, and this can only be done effectively in love guided by wisdom. A technique, or a particular school of metaphysical speculation, may be essential for us at a particular stage of our spiritual growth. But as soon as its presuppositions or consequences limit us in our ascent to God, it must be left behind, not in sorrow or anger, but rather in gratitude for what it has taught us about spiritual reality.

Of teachers

I have spoken several times about the importance of guidance on the spiritual path. It is a fact that there are natural mystics and spiritual directors, and part of the price they pay for the privilege of spiritual understanding is to guide and encourage others less advanced than themselves in knowledge on the path. In meditation, and especially in the practice of yoga, an experienced teacher is essential. He must be aware of the psychological effects of spiritual unfoldment—and here an understanding of modern depth psychology is useful—and also be able to discern psychic invasions into the personality so that he can guide the aspirant through the snare of the psychic to the full light of the spiritual. As I have said, not all psychic phenomena are to be deprecated—some are of great value—but it requires the gift of discernment of spirits to see which influences are beneficial and which are stultifying. The ignorance of most of those engaged in psychotherapy and psychiatry about the psychic part of man's nature, coupled with the deep fear felt by most priests, make this important subject taboo in the very quarters where a person possessed of psychic powers would naturally turn for guidance. A spiritual director cannot afford to be ignorant in these matters; indeed, if he is a true guide, he will almost certainly have had personal experience of the psychic field of existence.

A genuine teacher never vaunts himself. He is humble and unobtrusive. He does not overwhelm other people with evidence of psychic powers. Thus he does not read into the past or the future nor indulge in criticisms from a seat of authority. While he may indeed possess gifts of clairvoyance and precognition, he does not use them for his own exaltation in the eyes of others. The reality he sees is, in any case, far beyond the range of psychism. What concerns him is the aspirant's attitude to life, how he is bearing the burdens that life thrusts on him, and the way the personality is integrating around the focal point of the soul. He can assess the quality of meditation experienced by the disciple by the power of concentration manifested in the day-to-day affairs of life. And he can guide the disciple into greater depths of silence in which the still voice of God is heard. A real teacher is not interested in signs and wonders. He is concerned about the spiritual awakening of mankind. He knows that only when the kingdom of God is realised in the person can signs and wonders naturally proceed from him. And at this stage they lose their glamorous impact.

A teacher should not be actively approached from afar, for the person thus selected is almost certain to be the wrong one. The law is well known, "When the pupil is ready, the master appears." His appearance is often so casual as to appear fortuitous, but the impact he makes on the soul of the aspirant speaks of deep truth. The teacher, like any other human being, is not infallible, but the particular gift he has to offer is the one which the aspirant needs at that stage of his progress.

A special type of teacher is the guru. In the approach to God some people require a relationship of absolute dedication to a spiritually exalted person, in whom they see the divine essence and through whom alone they can reach a knowledge of God. Its advocates have no doubt that, except in such a dedicated attachment, the aspirant cannot proceed further along the spiritual path. The truth of the matter lies in all probability somewhere between a complete disregard for human teachers and an absolute dependence on them. For those of a very devotional temperament the presence of a guru is no doubt necessary until such time as the teacher can evoke those inner powers of discernment by which the disciple's spiritual advancement can occur independently of human aid. For others of a more independent nature such an intense attachment is quite alien. In their path they will come upon those more advanced in understanding than they are, and these teachers will act as beacons of enlightenment and encouragement, but such aspirants will see beyond personal attachment to any one teacher. To me this is the healthier path, especially for those who recognise the supremacy of Christ (both cosmic and incarnate) and are tractable to the guidance of the Holy Spirit within them. A teacher, or spiritual director, should aim at making a disciple so integrated within himself that he can respond positively to the Holy Spirit.

The danger of devotion to any human source of knowledge is that of fundamentalism. Whatever the guru teaches is taken as the truth, and the aspirant merely exchanges a scriptural or ecclesiastical authority for a personal one. As elsewhere, we cannot accept any second-hand knowledge as the truth. It has to be proved by the experience that comes to us as we live purposefully and dangerously.

Of communities

The religious community is an integral part of several religious traditions, notably Buddhism and Catholic Christianity. Here a group of people are united in the quest for reality at the cost of personal comfort or worldly advancement. The life is austere, and the religious exercises observed keep the mind fixed on the source of being, to which the creature moves in selfless dedication. But the most taxing part of the monastic life is the resolution of personal tensions. In close communion with others of differing temperaments, it is impossible to remain detached from the impingement of hostile psychic forces that arise from within oneself no less than from others around one. No secrets can be hidden in this closely related group, and the wounding realisation of one's inadequacy can make life very difficult. We learn from this that life is a constant relationship, or as Martin Buber puts it; "All real living is meeting."

Can a group of people work in a rather less formalised type of community, one in which the religious element is less dominant and outer relationships in the world are more cultivated? This is one of the problems of people who are united in a common quest for the good life, but do not necessarily all belong to a single religious tradition. There have been many attempts at establishing such communities over the centuries. The common link has varied from an idealistic type of socialism to a vegetarian theosophical metaphysic. In the end non-religious communities tend to disintegrate. One cannot form a closed group of any permanence except under the leadership of God. Thus the well-tried religious communities are unlikely to be superseded.

But there should be a place also for dedicated workers in the world, unbound by external vows and not necessarily unmarried, to live in close communion with each other. Whether this is an enclosed area of land or whether they live separately in the secular city is not of fundamental importance. The essential requirement is that they should be in close contact with each other, so that they can work as a team. Indeed, this concept of a community is less exclusive than the traditional one, for the members are also in close relationship with the world and its needs. The inner group could meet at regular intervals for meditation, prayer, and a domestic Eucharist, or equivalent sacrament, depending on the religious tradition of those participating. It seems likely that intimate groups of this type will be the foundation of the church of the future. In such a group there might be that love which is the basis of real spiritual communion, a love so obviously absent from most conventional church services. If love flourished among groups of people in a domestic setting, it would radiate from them to others who might then be brought, by their own desire, into this intimate communion. In such a manner more and more people would be made aware of the abiding nature of God's love as revealed in human relationships, and the divine community might really be established through a willed effort.

The spiritual path

The spiritual path embraces the whole of life. The discipline of relationships within a difficult community is as much part of the ascent of the mind to God as is the time set aside for prayer. Every work done with single-minded purpose, with an intent concentration, is a spiritual exercise. If one's mode of living leads to impaired efficiency in the work at hand or if it results in a neglect of personal relationships, it is not spiritually based no matter how frequently it is punctuated by meditation or embellished with inner experiences.

The spiritual life should also be a fruitful life in the world—fruitful not so much in acquiring the good things of life for oneself as in making these more available to other people. The type of person who never really achieves anything practical and depends for his existence on the support of his friends is no credit to the spiritual life. On the contrary, he would be a support for his weaker brethren if his life were truly spiritually based. The realised mystic is the most practical of men because of his widened vision and greater freedom of self-expression. In addition, he can relate more easily to a greater variety of people than can the materially based person.

The fruit of spirituality is joy—a constant joy in every situation. For the earth is good, and life is worth while despite its many dark moments. The present suffering is in no way to be compared with the glory that is to be revealed in us. This great insight of St. Paul is the result of faith made real by mystical illumination.

The great mystics of the world have all had first-class minds. Think of the Buddha and Shankara in the Eastern tradition or St. Paul, Plotinus, St. Augustine, Meister Eckhart, St. John of the Cross, and Jakob Boehme in the West. This does not mean that only the intellectual type of person can aspire to mystical illumination. The mind that is tractable to illumination is one that is well trained and proficient in practical life. Arid intellectualism is a barrier to mystical experience. Nevertheless, mysticism yields its most valuable fruit when the experience can be interpreted and brought into a living framework by a well-trained reasoning mind.

In no area of life is the balance between intuition and intellect more important than in the interpretation of mystical experience. Thus the disciple should take every opportunity of broadening his mind by keeping abreast of new developments in the various fields of human endeavour. A blinding revelation of divine truth can be made visible to the remainder of the world by the intellectual proficiency of the mystic.

We turn finally to the main task of life, the building of the body that matters most, the spiritual body.

CHAPTER 17

Building the spiritual body

THE ULTIMATE PURPOSE OF our life on earth is to lay the founda-
tions of a spiritual body of such excellence that it will continue
our existence after the earthly body is cast off. In other words,
the object of earthly life is spiritual reality. There is in fact only
one existence, and this is eternal life. But our painstaking work
in the world of limitation is a preparation for the realisation of
eternity in every moment of life. In the midst of life we are in
death. Indeed, every new experience is a little death to a past,
cherished belief. The relinquishing of old concepts and ways of
life before the challenge of new insights is the way of death
during earthly life. And if we persist in faith, we find that the
death is also the gateway to a new life. It is in this frame of
reference that we can consider best the problem of death, which
is the true end of all earthly experience.

What is the most important thing we have to achieve while on
earth? Is it material gain—which we have to relinquish and pass
on to others? Is it power and prestige—which drop from us as
soon as we lose authority over others? Is it intellectual knowledge
—which is superseded by new developments almost before the
world has had time to assess our own contribution? Is it physical
pleasure—with the body ageing from its very moment of birth?
No, none of these can be the great work of man, though each is
important in its own right in helping to integrate the personality
within the wider context of the world. But as an end in itself,
neither gain, nor power, nor knowledge, nor pleasure, can suffice,
because all of these are submerged in the finality of bodily death.
There is only one thing that can survive personal death, and that
is love. For in love we are no longer circumscribed, finite units,

but are members one of another. Each little death is the ending of an enclosed view of identity. As we lose that dominating concern for ourselves, our opinions, and the justification to retain our personal image in the world, which characterises worldly man, so we move into a new understanding of reality.

We prepare for death as soon as we are born. The essential feature of the preparation is a graded sacrifice of the enclosed self for the wider vision of concern for others. As a spiritually advancing man grows older, so he welcomes each passing year with open arms. Age, the terrible threat to the immature person who clings desperately on to the last vestiges of receding youth, is the great friend of the spiritual man. Each year brings him closer to truth, and enables him to discard more of the superficial dross of outer personality—or rather to transmute that dross into the material of the soul.

It follows therefore that man's great work while in the flesh is the forging of relationships. It is by these that the spiritual body is built while on earth, so that when the mortal body is cast off, it will be alive to contain the soul in its onward journey through time into eternity. As we grow older, the power, the importance, the pleasure of the body, the material affluence that we guarded so carefully, all become past memories. Indeed, it is a measure of our spiritual status while on earth just how much time we spend in memories of past grandeur and in private fantasies of no practical application. We are indeed already dead, in the conventional use of that word, if our lives cling to the past or to delusions that keep us from reality. We are truly alive when we can, by an act of will, bid farewell in tender decisiveness to the past and to our inner vain imaginings, and face the future in clear-headed contemplation. But the one aspect of life that does not pass into oblivion is that of relationships. For as we give of ourselves increasingly to others, so they become part of our lives. As we fail, so they care for us as we, in our time, cared for others when they were low.

This caring is not a mere duty forced on us by mutual social advantage. It is a deep concern which is of the nature of love. As I have stressed so often already, as we open ourselves to the adventure of knowing others, so God reveals Himself to us and shows us our own true nature, which is of Him. The soul is not merely a focus of personal identity. It is also a shared possession of all life, and through it we are in psychic communion with all that exists. The mystic knows of this truth in its more embracing reality, while the psychically aware person gets glimpses of it through extrasensory perception of other souls both those living in the world and those existing in the greater world of the life eternal.

The event of physical death is an awesome moment. There is no absolute proof of survival of any aspect of the personality. While the data of psychical research are not negligible, and indeed spiritualists are convinced that they can enjoy meaningful communication with the deceased, there is a veil between the living and those who have passed beyond mortal life which has not yet been successfully penetrated by objective means. This to me is exactly as it should be. Until we have reached the spiritual stature of Christ, the full meaning of resurrection and immortality will be hidden from us. The awe of death and the uncertainty of personal survival are the foundation on which the corner-stones of faith are laid. Ultimately survival at death is as personal an experience as is survival at birth from our mother's womb. In the life of separation, we have to undergo many trials alone. Our friends can support us and remember us in their prayers, but we alone can do the deed and experience the consequences. And yet it is in going alone on the inevitable journey to completion that we begin to realise that we are not really alone at all. We are supported by the unseen hosts of eternity, amongst whom are our earthly friends in the form of immortal souls—a form of a different magnitude from that by which we knew them in everyday life. This is the inner meaning of intercessory prayer, to which is added the communion of those many souls who have entered the greater life beyond the grave.

As we move from earthly life to the unknown, yet dimly experienced, realm beyond death, so we put aside all the things that we held dear during life. Our mortal work is done, our possessions must now be taken over by those who follow us, and our relationships of a personal nature limited by the range of the five external senses fade from our view. We have nothing left but our own identity. Everything that we identified ourselves by in the world of matter has been removed from us. We stand naked and alone. At last we know what is real and eternal and what was transitory and changing. This is the moment in which we exchange spiritual reality for mortal life. But who is to receive us into the new realm of being? We have been cleared of the past nexus of events by which we have identified ourselves, and are naked in a new darkness—dark because the way is not by earthly sight. A new light is to be revealed to the emergent personality, the light of love.

It is here that we understand how important our past life in the world has been. We are received into the greater life by those friends whom we received when we were living on earth. And I do not limit the friend only to those whom we knew and loved while on earth. This body of friends is much vaster than a mere reunion of past comrades on the mortal path. It includes the full communion of saints, provided we are fit to receive them. "Make to yourselves friends of the mammon of unrighteousness; that, when ye fail, they may receive you into everlasting habitations" (Luke 16.9).

It is the quiet, unobtrusive opening of ourselves to all manner of men in humble service—above all the service of simply giving them our attention—that brings its reward on the other side of life. It is not great intellectual knowledge, political power, material wealth, or physical strength that can forge an enduring relationship. All who pin their faith in these personal attributes will find themselves derelict when the physical body is no more, and when the money of the world can no longer buy anything. In the life of the greater world no secrets can be hidden, and all desires are known, for the concealing power of the physical body is no more, and the transparency of the spiritual body leaves no part of it protected from the knowledge and the scrutiny of the whole community of souls.

The traditional states of heaven and hell can be seen in this relationship. We are in hell, whether now on earth or on the other side of life, when we are immersed in ourselves. When our awareness cannot transcend self-interest, when our spiritual vision is so dim that we cannot see anyone outside ourselves, when our lives run in a rut of vain imaginings and futile fantasies, we are in hell. We are cut off from psychic communion with the greater community by our own self-centred attitude, and the life-giving power of the Holy Spirit is excluded from us. Until we, through openness to God's grace, can move beyond the little self to the soul in its eternal communion with all life, we cannot escape the darkness of hell.

Such hell is bad enough on this side of the grave, but it becomes increasingly fearful in the life beyond the grave, for the familiar landmarks of the earth—its solid structures and well-established connexions—are swallowed up in oblivion, and there is nothing left except the person and his confused awareness. Indeed, some personalities (they are now called discarnate entities) live in a private world of past fantasy, and may remain indefinitely unaware that they have passed into the greater world of life. In other words, they are not aware that they have died. Such a state of confusion is a fearful one, but it is related entirely to the attitude of the person himself. There is no question of punishment by God (or some other power). On the contrary, all the forces of light both in the world of matter (through prayers for the dead) and in the greater world beyond the grave are working in love towards the redemption of this "lost" person. This love shows itself as light, but it cannot penetrate into the awareness of the lost personality until it is open to change. Fortunately, through divine compassion an opening does occur in the fullness of the new life, and then the personality loses its old restricted ways of thought and enters into the greater life around it. This dedication of self to life is the meaning of heaven. It is with us, at least potentially, here on earth when we are doing our work properly, and it becomes even more radiant in the greater life when we move beyond the restriction of the physical body to the openness and vitality of the spiritual body.

The soul and the spiritual body

What is it that survives the immediate death of the physical body? Of course, to the atheistic humanist this question is pitiful, for since to him matter alone is real, there can be no survival of anything resembling a conscious personality once the brain has disintegrated. But to those of us who have cultivated an inner life of meditation and prayer while here on earth, and have lived in self-giving relationship (relationship in depth, as the phrase goes) with others, especially our loved ones, the introspective fact of an inner identity, or soul, becomes ever clearer. If we are psychically attuned, sporadic episodes of telepathy, precognition, or out-of-the-body experiences will make the dualism of mind and body—a position detested by most psychologists and many philosophers because of its far-reaching implications against the materialist orthodoxies of our time—ever more credible. Such a view does not deny the importance of the physical body while we are alive on earth. Indeed, incarnation is to be seen as the training ground of the mind and soul in the limitation of the matter of the body. If the body is not functioning properly, the mind becomes increasingly impotent, a tragic situation seen especially when there is damage to the brain. And the potentiality of matter is quickened by the mind—in this sentence lies the heart of the mystery of the resurrection of the body.

But when the time comes for the physical body to return to elements of the earth from which it was fashioned and nourished, the mind-soul personality is released in a world outside the limitation of space and time by which we live our earthly lives. This mind-soul personality is loosely called the "spirit" especially by spiritualists, but it is not to be confused with the spark, or apex, of the soul by which the fact of God is known. The whole mind-soul complex is the spiritual body, and it has been built from our experiences and attitudes during physical life. In theosophical thought (derived as part of the ageless wisdom from Eastern religion and metaphysics) a series of "bodies" are envisaged as ensheathing the soul (which itself is the body of the spirit). While I would not deny this possibility, and indeed am personally sympathetic to this theory, I do not regard it as vitally important in one's understanding of survival of death. It is an added embellishment which must be accepted only as it is revealed to you.

The spiritual body, at the time of its separation from the disintegrating physical body, consists essentially of the mental, emotional, and aspirational qualities of the whole person to whom it formerly belonged. In other words at the time of death the mental part of the personality is not greatly changed, and indeed in people of low spiritual stature this trivial level of mental reality may persist indefinitely. But in those of spiritual awareness, the mental and emotional side of the personality are rapidly shed—or more correctly are incorporated into the soul, which grows in comprehension and in greater union with reality. Spiritualistic communication, for which I myself am not an enthusiast, taps the superficial mental level of the personality of the deceased, and the material revealed is usually trivial and seldom progressive. At the level of the soul there is no communication through sensitives (or mediums), but rather a direct communion between lover and beloved.

I have, in these last two sentences, appeared to accept that mediumistic communication genuinely occurs between the minds of the discarnate and the worldly living. In fact, the source of much material is open to doubt. The greater portion is a simple reading of the sitter's mind by the medium (this is a fine example of telepathy), some is guess-work with an unconsciously fraudulent background, and some may be true communication with a discarnate source—whose credentials may sometimes be less impeccable than either the medium or the sitter realises. It is for this reason that one can seldom be enthusiastic about the material evoked by a medium, although many bereaved people gain great inner strength because of the evidence of survival (which is real enough to them) so provided.

It is often said that the existence of those who have passed on to the other side of life is so different in character that we cannot grasp it until we too have made the transition. This is largely true, but the personality of the deceased persists for a variable period of time (using this word in the earthly context), and an important part of post-mortem existence is the reliving of past experiences of earth. The great spiritual law that as a man sows so shall he reap is obeyed. But we are the judge of our own past When the soul is finally released, it can see how great were its shortcomings, and also how difficult were the circumstances of earthly life under which it laboured. It is now much more tractable to the love of God than it was on earth, enclosed in a dense, physical body.

The hope that, in the after-life, we may meet Christ face to face, while in one way rather too naïve to be the full truth, is nevertheless accurate inasmuch as the naked soul is far more aware of the cosmic dimensions of Christ than is the incarnate soul. The life in the world to come starts as a mental construction. The truth of one's attitude and behaviour while on earth is pitilessly revealed, but as one comes more to oneself, one is immersed in the glorious beauty of a mental realm. This is called "heaven" or "summerland", and is to be contrasted with the greyness of the immediate post-mortem period (which is called "hell" or "hades"—into which Jesus descended after the crucifixion in order to release these sombre personalities from the bondage of spiritual darkness).

Esotericists speak of an etheric body that enshrouds the spiritual body during the period of darkness, and of its dissolution as the spiritual body is released into the light of heaven. Such a view is somewhat conditioned by earthly concepts of shrouds and bodies, and it might be easier simply to say that the personality comes to itself and acts more as it should have done while incarnate.

The heavenly state is a mental realm. It has no real substance, and is described as astral by esotericists, who also accept the presence of an astral body which limits the progress of the soul, until this body too is dissolved, and the soul reaches a more mystical level of reality. Personally I accept much of this, not merely because it is part of traditional teaching but because I have had direct, though fleeting, contact with what I believe are other realms of life. The one thing that has been brought forcibly to my attention is the mental, subjective existence of those who are newly deceased. They learn things too wonderful for us here to fathom, but they do not grow.

I have likened the immediate after-life to the discussion that follows an examination, in which we all partly pass and partly fail (in some instances the failure or the success strongly dominates). In this atmosphere we can sum up our merits and our faults, but we can in no way alter the result of the test, which is the life we have led on earth. All the understanding that we may have acquired in the vast timeless realm of the soul in communion with God has eventually to be put into practice once more in the less expansive, more restricted world of time and space, just as we have to sit the same, or else a more advanced, examination in due course depending on how we have fared in the present test.

The type of eternal bliss that is promised the devout religionist would be real hell if it were a fact. Life is growth into the fullness of being, and the means at hand are always relationships. There can be no real meaning in a realm of timeless, spaceless eternity, nor can there be growth in love where there is nothing to give away or sacrifice. It is fatuous to believe that the soul of any one of us, as we expire on our deathbed, is so advanced in perfection that it could enter the timeless realm of bliss (Nirvana in the Buddhist tradition) eternally. And who would choose bliss for himself while the whole creation groans as if in the pangs of childbirth? The law of life is rebirth, which means a dying to some part of one's previous attitude to reality. The soul is reborn into successive states of limitation, so that it can grow into something of the measure of the stature of the fullness of Christ. The forgiveness made plain in the atonement of Christ leaves all who accept this on the level of selfless love free to continue the quest unburdened by past guilt and regret ("Come unto me, all ye that labour and are heavy laden, and I will give you rest." —St. Matthew 11.28). But the path is one of patient toil, selfless giving, and dangerous living. There are no short cuts or magical escapes. The magic of the world lies in its very existence. He who can see no miracle in the constant fecundity of life will never see it if the order is changed.

Reincarnation

Mention of rebirth at once brings in the possibility of reincarnation, the assumption by the soul of a fresh physical body on successive occasions. Indeed, some people would equate the two words, but I prefer to speak of rebirth, an event that occurs continually during all phases of life whether here on earth or in the greater world beyond the grave. What realms of limitation the soul voluntarily accepts in its growth towards eternal union with God are not known ("in my Father's house are many mansions." St. John 14.12), and it would be presumptuous to assume that our little planet amid the countless galaxies of the cosmos is the only place of growth for the soul (nor need growth always take place on a strictly material plane). However, it seems likely that many souls do assume an earthly body on a number of occasions in their spiritual journey. The evidence of psychical research workers who have investigated the detailed memories of very young children—too young to have gleaned the information during their brief sojourn on earth—does bear out the theory that they had been incarnate in another human form not long before their present birth. This type of evidence is much more convincing than the alleged—and usually glamorous—memories of past lives on earth displayed by psychically attuned adults. In these cases the possibility of "cryptamnesia"—the sudden recall of a long submerged memory probably acquired during early childhood—can seldom be ruled out.

Reincarnation should not be confused with the transmigration of souls into animal bodies. This is, at most, extremely improbable because of the complex nature of the human mind-soul complex (the spiritual body). It could hardly function in the limited brain of other animals, and therefore it would not learn by growth in relationships.

A great snare in all rebirth hypotheses, and especially in relation to reincarnation, is the penal attitude adopted to present difficulties. A harshly moralistic approach attributes present tragedies to past errors and speaks dogmatically of each person working out his own "karma"—a word which simply means action. In this context it would imply a payment of past debts, a reaping of what we have sown in a past life of selfish action or personal betrayal. But life is not as rigidly moralistic as this. In Christ we grow beyond bondage to the law of cause and effect, and live by love. Every difficulty the aspiring person has to meet is to be seen not as a consequence for wrong action in the past, but as the necessary tension for growth of the personality in the future. If this attitude of holy indifference to the world's concepts of success and failure is achieved (by God's grace), we cease to be ensnared in detailed considerations of the mechanism of rebirth or the working out of old scores between people, and live more fully in the moment. Thus a spiritually aware person, while not denying the purifying effect of life's past experiences, lives in the present. He will accept a rebirth hypothesis as the most logical solution to the personal tragedies we all have to undergo, the birth of mentally subnormal children who can never achieve much in that particular life, and the glowing brilliance of childhood genius. But he moves beyond considerations of the working out of justice in individual life to the contemplation of the unity of all men in God.

The soul grows through successive experiences. The reasoning mind and emotional response that characterise the personality are not discarded in the longer view of the after-life. They are incorporated in the soul. Their personal memories are so fused with the awareness of the soul that their contribution enhances its range and comprehension. If rebirth, as I have portrayed it, is a fact—and agnosticism remains a duty until a personal revelation expands one's awareness—the only aspect of a past life that is worth remembering is that relating to our moral nature. The categorical imperative of Kant—which is categorical only to aspiring people—could well be the fruit of past experience of the soul incarcerated in a selfish personality. It is an empirical fact that the golden rule—do to others as you would have them do to you—comes only with long experience of the world and the suffering inherent in that experience. Compassion is the fruit of longsuffering, a suffering that is part of all limitation in a time-space world.

I am not therefore impressed by the grandiose reincarnational memories claimed by some enthusiasts. To them each affront has a past background, and each reverse is the paying back of a karmic debt. If this were the way of the soul's progress, we would never move away from the realm of personal revenge. Until we see every aspect of life, pleasant and unpleasant alike, as part of the soul's growing into communion with all life in God we are not fully alive and our spiritual vision is faulty. Christ is the prototype of all the saints who have suffered grievously in this life for the benefit of their fellows in all generations. "Greater love hath no man than this, that a man give up his life for his friend." (St. John 15.13.) If we could see rebirth in this exalted context, we would cease to be absorbed in trivialities about past actions and future recompense.

Survival of the spiritual body

What I have written above is a personal confession of faith. But like all real faith it is based on inner experience, and is not simply a fresh presentation of Christian theology on to which is grafted aspects of the ageless wisdom (or perennial philosophy, as it is more usually called). The reader must use his own spiritual discernment and accept or reject it for himself.

There is no scientifically acceptable proof of survival of death. The reason for this, as we shall see in the final chapter, is the ill-defined quality of personal identity. It is an act of faith to accept the identity of someone you "know" when he communicates with you by telephone or the written word. How do you know he is not an impostor? An inner discernment provides the confidence of identity without which normal social intercourse would be impossible. But when the same person passes beyond mortal life, his whole personality is bound to alter rapidly in the new environment of freedom. Direct communication can no longer be sensory, but must be extrasensory, or telepathic. If a third person, the medium, is also implicated in the transaction, his (or more likely her) personality impinges and further distorts the communication. Some of the pitfalls of mediumship I have already mentioned. Extrasensory contact with a living source who knew the deceased person is the most important.

True communion with the deceased is a spiritual act. In the parable of Lazarus and the rich man, we are told that if the living will not hear Moses and the prophets, they will not be persuaded of the reality of the after-life, even if one were to rise from the dead (Luke 16. 19-31). This is the truth. A generation seeking after signs and wonders before it accepts spiritual reality will never be satisfied. Each sign will be analysed away, and a suitable materialistic explanation will be found that can lull the unbelieving into a dogmatic sleep once more.

The history of spiritualism and psychical research is an eloquent testimony to this truth. Spiritual facts can be discerned only by the Holy Spirit in man. Until we are tractable to the Holy Spirit our faith will be a paltry thing. When Christ appeared after the Resurrection, it was only to His friends that He showed Himself. He did not appear to those who had condemned and crucified Him, although such a presentation could hardly have failed to shake them out of their unbelief. But He never aimed at forcing people to be other than themselves. His was the way of freedom, not coercion. The disciples, weak men as they had been during the passion of their Master, were nevertheless sufficiently advanced spiritually to bear the fact of the resurrection. They were the fathers of the new dispensation when the Holy Spirit dwelt fully with them.

In all ages He has come to men of all conditions and religious traditions (St. Paul's experience is the prototype of many later conversions) as a blinding revelation—the revelation of supreme mystical experience. This is the moment of truth when the veil between the world of matter and the world of unseen reality is finally dissolved, and they are found to be one. He who has had the veil dissolved by divine grace accepts the fact of survival and the meaning of immortality.

So to immortality and resurrection we now turn.

CHAPTER 18

Immortality and resurrection

IF THE SCHEME OF survival of personality is anything like I have portrayed, it is evident that the soul is the permanent factor and that the mental, emotional, and physical elements are added during the process of its incarnation. The physical body is cast off at death, and the emotional and intellectual aspects of personality, while persisting for a variable period after the death of the physical body and being sometimes the means of meaningful communication with the living, are gradually lost also. I personally do not believe they are simply discarded, as is the earthly body, but are incorporated into the soul to form a growing spiritual body. Traces of their memory remain in some people and give rise to the belief in a past existence. As I mentioned in the last chapter, there are well attested instances of very small children having arresting memories of a recent past life, memories that have been investigated and confirmed by competent psychical research workers (the name of Professor Ian Stevenson of the American Society for Psychical Research is particularly relevant in this respect, and his book *Twenty Cases Suggestive of Reincarnation* is a model of painstaking, objective analysis). It is interesting that these children cease to be concerned with these past memories as they grow up, and by adolescence they are so well integrated into their present environment that they have all but forgotten them.

The soul itself is both an individual unit and an integral part of the created cosmos. In other words, while my soul is unique because of the particular experiences it has undergone in this life (and who can say how many previous lives, whether on earth or elsewhere, for its pre-existence seems to me to be quite as probable as its survival and growth in a future state), it acquires its authenticity and meaning by being in corporate unity with all other souls, which are the matrix of the created universe. The fact of soul pervades all life. All sentient creatures have some aspect of soul in them (some philosophers see mind even in the inanimate world, for example Teilhard de Chardin, and I sympathise with this mystical point of view), and in man the soul acquires the autonomy which is the supreme glory of humanity. This shows itself in a freed will, a will directly under the control of the soul and working in the direction of unity with all souls and with God, who has created the soul through the agency of the cosmic Christ and the Holy Spirit. Thus the individual soul reaches its fullness of being when it has passed from individuality to unity with other souls. But this union is not a fusion or an incorporation, for each soul retains its own identity in unity.

Of course, the very concept of soul is beyond the range of the unaided reason. It requires that peculiar mystical apprehension that can accept contradictions as all being true within a wider context of synthesis. Aristotelian logic, which is the basis of scientific method, is transcended by mystical intuition (as indeed it is in the speculations of modern theoretical physics in which a single elementary particle can function alternatively as a quantum and a wave). The soul is most fully itself when it is no longer itself in isolation, but is one with the whole soul matrix of the universe. In this one can begin to glimpse the meaning of the Buddha's doctrine of "anatta", or no soul. The concept of separate identity is meaningless in mystical reality except in the context of corporate unity. The Pauline teaching about the Body of Christ is a Christian insight of parallel value—of what validity is an eye or a foot severed from the body of which it is a part? It can be dissected and analysed, but has no further intrinsic use. It may be that each individual soul is created from the undifferentiated matrix of soul throughout time, for creation is not static. It continues throughout time until all is perfect in God. On the physical level this is seen in the process of evolution, now generally accepted by scientists and also by such theologians as Teilhard de Chardin and A. N. Whitehead. It would seem that the work of the created individual soul is to attain union with God by its own free will, and not as an automatic process. The way it attains this union is by its experience in the limitation of time and space, and by its redemption, or resurrection, of the material universe. On earth (and we can speak of no other mode of finite existence in our present state of knowledge) man is the most highly evolved being, and the soul is in charge of a wonderfully potent organism. Its action, as we have already seen, is to integrate the body, reasoning mind, and emotional nature to the stature of a mature person. If it fails to act well, as is in varying degree the rule, a poorly integrated person emerges, and his life is in one way or another consummated in futility. His spiritual body is a paltry thing, and future work in a rebirth sequence is necessary before he can aspire to something of the nature of Christ. However, the natural tendency of the soul appears to be towards union with its own and this tendency lays it open to the grace of God, without which there could be no progress. But if the soul is granted free will, it is conceivable that it might choose the path of destruction, or evil, rather than that of resurrection, or good. It might indeed deliberately choose to exclude itself from the love of God. Certainly some of the parables in the Gospel stress this possibility, and the lives of atrociously evil men who have killed millions of people and reduced whole civilisations to desolation are a constant reminder of the terrible power of evil, a power that is essentially negative in that it denies all life and leads to complete annihilation. In this case, the soul might forfeit its identity and return to the matrix from which it was created.

Personally I believe in the ultimate redemption of all creation in the love of God. I look for a final restitution in which every creature will return to God. Here I follow the theology of the greater hope glimpsed by St. Paul, (1 Corinthians 15.28 and Colossians 1.20), cherished by Origen and St. Gregory of Nyssa, revealed to Dame Julian of Norwich, and taught by William Law in his later life. This is the meaning of immortality, and the scheme outlined, though no doubt unduly well defined in the face of the ignorance that is our common lot in this world of becoming, stresses the importance of every moment of earthly life in the growth of the soul into a knowledge of eternity. I see evil as a psychic residue derived from the selfish actions of men, and no doubt also other modalities of being (such as the angelic order), from the beginning of the process of creation. While evil has no substantive existence, it can be used by depraved beings and lead to general destruction. It would seem that the darkness is as much a part of the divine creation as the light, and that the soul's work is to transmute its energy from destructiveness to resurrection.

The resurrection of the body is the reverse side of the immortality of the soul. The two proceed together. Indeed, immortality is of little importance apart from the resurrection that accompanies it. Resurrection of the body is not to be interpreted as a crude raising up of the long deceased, disintegrated physical body at the "last day", so that the body and soul can come together again. It is to be understood as a raising up of the heaviness and dullness of the earth into a new life of spiritual vibrancy. The transfiguration of Christ is a demonstration of the quickening of the flesh of a spiritual master, and it was a prelude to the remarkable resurrection experiences that followed His death. The body that appeared had qualities of movement and dissolution quite unlike those of a normal physical body. The resurrection appearances are an unsolved problem. It may be that they merely represented mystical experiences on the part of the disciples, or they may have been genuine materialisations of the etheric body that is said to enshroud the spiritual body immediately after death. But the third possibility seems the most likely, namely a transmutation of the physical body directly into its spiritual counterpart by the enlightened soul. If this is the truth, as I personally believe it to be, it would seem that in the instance of the resurrection the physical body of Jesus contributed to His glorious spiritual body. When lesser people die there is no evidence of a similar transmutation of their bodies, but at least we can look for an intellectual and emotional resurrection. And in the fullness of time perhaps a transmuted physical body will enrich the world, and also the soul of the person. Thus resurrection in its most exalted context means the raising up of the transient physical world into a knowledge of the timeless splendour of eternity. Flesh and blood cannot inherit the kingdom of God, but in Christ all is raised from the transience of corruption to the eternity of spiritual existence. Thus everything corrupt, unwholesome, ugly, and evil is capable of being redeemed by love. I would go further, and affirm my belief in the ultimate resurrection of all earthly, finite things so that they may return to God, the source of all creation, renewed and glorified.

This is surely the meaning of our life. We are to grow progressively into the knowledge of God's love, and we do this by giving of ourselves unreservedly to the work of the world at hand. We cannot rise until we help others to rise with us. Who would want an ascent to the realm of permanent mystical illumination while there was even one unredeemed creature in the world? This is the meaning of love, and the reason why a person of love cannot bear to contemplate the absolute destruction of any soul. Condemnation melts away before a greater affirmation of the sacredness of all life. Nothing, no matter how evil, is beyond the redeeming love of God, which may radiate from a redeemed man.

The identity of the individual would, according to this scheme of existence, be a union of the soul, which in all probability existed before his present conception in his mother's womb, and the mind-body complex that is acquired from the circumstances of his incarnation. Thus we inherit much of our personality from our ancestors, and especially our parents, while the environment in which we are reared produces far-reaching effects on that personality.

The identity of a person is indeed vast. And as he grows in the spiritual life, his soul enlarges in comprehension and unites consciously with the souls of others in close spiritual fellowship. The formation of the group-soul, an event that is now assuming great importance in the lives of aspirants to God, is the presage of that far-off, yet well-remembered, day when all creatures will return in love through the Son by whom all things were made, to the Father. At this stage the claims of a private, personal identity will become irrelevant, for we shall love our neighbour as ourself, realising at last that we are our neighbour.

This realisation of union with mankind will herald the consummation of the marriage of man with God. At this point, rebirth will be transcended in a state of mystical unity called Nirvana by the Buddhists, and which is so splendid that it cannot be described in words.

Epilogue

It may seem somewhat out of place to end a book on life with metaphysical speculations about eternity. But physical life is ultimately meaningless except in the context of eternal life, and eternal life cannot be a viable proposition unless there is survival of some part of the personality after physical death. As Jung remarks in the penultimate chapter of his autobiography *Memories, Dreams, Reflections,* everyone should form some conception of life after death. To have failed to do so is a great loss. Indeed, I would add that to hope for some working-out of this life's experiences is the height of reason.

To anticipate annihilation is not stoical courage but irresponsible folly, for it negates on a larger scale those very qualities that men of all traditions hold most dear. If we live spiritually now, we can accept the summons to eternal life in every action we perform. And when the night comes in which we can do no further earthly work, the light of the Spirit will reveal new realms of exploration into the being of God.

Index